A New Cold War

The Prophecies of Nostradamus, Stormberger and Edgar Cayce

Other Books by John Hogue

Predictions for 2014
Predictions for 2013-2014
Nostradamus: The War with Iran
Nostradamus: The End of End Times
Nostradamus and the Antichrist, Code Named: Mabus
Messiahs: The Visions and Prophecies for the Second Coming
The Last Pope: The Decline and Fall of the Church of Rome
The Millennium Book of Prophecy
Nostradamus: The Complete Prophecies
1000 for 2000 Startling Predictions for the New Millennium
Nostradamus: The New Millennium
The Last Pope "Revisited"
The Essential Nostradamus
Nostradamus: A Life and Myth
Kamikaze Tomorrowland (a ScryFy Short Story)

A New Cold War

The Prophecies of Nostradamus, Stormberger and Edgar Cayce

John Hogue

Acclaim for John Hogue:

"John Hogue's *A New Cold War* is a masterpiece of prophecy."

—**Whitley Strieber**, author of *Communion* and
The Coming Global Superstorm with Art Bell

THE NEW COLD WAR
Predictions of Nostradamus, Stormberger and Edgar Cayce
Published by John Hogue
Copyright © 25 July 2014 by HogueProphecy Publishing
All rights reserved.

ISBN-13: 9781501081514
ISBN-10: 1501081519

Cover: John Hogue, Gail LaForest

Dedication

To the music of Dmitri Shostakovich that foresaw, through the witness of a symphonic language higher than words, the great wars and revolutions, past "and" future.

Acknowledgments

Thanks to my conceptual editor, Francis Perry, my copy and proofing editor, Gail LaForest and also Brian Ghilliotti for his Stormberger research assistance. And finally, thanks to Vipassana: a meditation and a mother all in *oneness*.

Table Of Contents

Introduction:
With Open Eyes Blind

True Prophecy anticipates the unexpected and the unplanned-for *unbelievable*. It's 14 April 2014. I begin my tale of future time on the 102nd anniversary of the sinking of RMS "Titan" on 14 April 1912. Perhaps you think I've misnamed the ship sunk by an iceberg off the coast of Newfoundland. I'm merely sharing with you the first "report" published about the unsinkable-sunk RMS *Titanic*, logged in 1897 from the pen of fiction writer and former mariner, Morgan Robertson (1861-1915). Yes, the first accurate report was printed in a purely fictional account 15 years before it happened.

Robertson liked to "channel" his fictions onto paper, using what he called his "astral writing partner." In his mind, under glittering stars of a moonless night over black water came the ocean liner on her maiden voyage. Her three twisting screws churned a starlit path through the black surface, pushing her 75,000 tons at 25 knots. She was in a great hurry to steam from Britain to New York in record time, only the *Titan* was heading right into the path of an iceberg.

Robertson's astral oracle had given him the vision behind his closed eyes of that name appearing on the ocean liner's bow. Moreover, she "was" unsinkable, or so thought the 3,000 souls sailing upon her 800-foot length, safely residing in her cabins or promenading down her decks where underneath their feet was a series of 19 watertight compartments. Why then was there a need for lifeboats to congest one's evening stroll? A mere 24 of them was more than enough.

"Folly," impressed the astral messenger into Robertson's mind with an image of the Titan's collision with the iceberg and it sinking with a majority of its passengers: ship lights flickering out, fading into black waters.

He published his novel, *The Wreck of the Titan, or Futility* inadvertently reporting in fiction one of the greatest and most tragically iconic maritime disasters in history 15 years before many of the details became fact. For instance, on a moonless night in April 1912, the RMS *Titanic* on her *maiden voyage* cut the icy waters of the *North Atlantic* off Newfoundland. Her *three propellers* churned *66,000 tons* at *23 knots*, because her creators onboard were eager to break a North Atlantic crossing record, heedless of the risk, righteously ignorant of an unseen iceberg in the ocean liner's path.

Crew officers herded *2,223 passengers* into the frosty air. They waited their turn to crowd and then be lowered into icy Atlantic waters on one of only *twenty-two* available lifeboats! Yet why should there have been more? Hubris had declared this *883-foot* ocean liner iceberg proof. It had *16 watertight compartments*. Only three were sliced open by the iceberg, yet it was just enough to let water flow up and spill over one after another of 16 watertight compartment walls as there were no watertight passageways through the floors. A majority of her passengers faced an icy death on the *moonless night* of 14 *April* 1912.

If a soothsayer seeking your permission to publish his book of prophecies wrote that your husband was going to die from an unexpected sporting accident, you might call him on the carpet to explain himself. You might nag your jock of a spouse until he bends and he summons "this Nostradamus fellow" to court for an audience.

As for you, my dear king and husband, you don't have much interest in anything prophetic. You would rather be boar hunting on horseback with your mates on the palace grounds that afternoon than to sit in royal attendance with the wife and her bowing, fawning soothsaying bore. Indeed you *will* be off hunting as soon as you can excuse yourself. Pleasant and respectful though he is, you seem uncomfortable with all this prophesying and destiny stuff. You regard with lowered languorous eye the graying forked bear of the man in the three-cornered scholar's cap with the penetrating pale eyes. How he reminds you of your tiresome schoolmaster. Your bejeweled hand steadies a drooping, sleepy chin and you think, "Let me out of this stuffy place, into the parklands, under the Sun. I want to shoot an arrow at something!"

The price of a very public 10-year affair with Diane de Poitiers required Henri II, King of France, gracefully tolerate his Italian-born Queen Catherine de Medici's passion for parading yet another augur or conjuror for a "look what the cat drug in" audience when it concerned some fickle finger of *La Fortuna* pointed at your person and the survival of the Valois dynasty.

"Here we are again," muses the king. "First her fellow, native Florentine forecaster, Luc Gauricus, now this Nostradamus fellow, this drawling Provencal author of astrological almanacs, whom the queen is no doubt among the first to read."

The queen wants her king to listen carefully and consider how clearly this author of cloudy quatrain verses picks up Gauricus' thread about a future accident where he's killed in a jousting tournament. She designs to fascinate as much as frighten her lord into abandoning the sport.

Henry remained serenely noncommittal about what dire fortune awaited him with lances and lists. He told the Captain of his Scottish Guards, Gabriel de Larges, Comte de Montgomery: "I care not if my death be in that manner more than in any other," adding, "I would even prefer it, to die by the hand of whoever he might be, so long as he was brave and valiant and that I kept my honor."

The audience Nostradamus attended before King Henri and Queen Catherine focused on a prophecy resembling Gauricus' vision. There was no way the two seers could have known each other. Catherine had pressed her prince to bring the mage of Salon, Provence, to court in August 1555. This happened a month after the Royal Library in Paris, had given the first serialized installment of his history of the future approval for publication in the realm. Catherine de Medici may have read the first volume of *Les Propheties* before anyone else, she had agents in the library ever on the hunt for new occult tomes. Thereafter, the quatrain indexed [Century] 1 Q [quatrain] 35 in volume one of *Les Propheties* by Michel de Nostradamus had become the talk of French court.

1 Q35

The young lion will overcome the older one
On the field of combat in single battle:
He will pierce his eyes through a golden cage
Two wounds made one, then he dies a cruel death.

Readers of the verses at court believed the "lions" were two warriors, a younger one pitted against the elder who was the king. Did not Henri arm himself for a tournament bearing his lion-embossed shield? *Single combat* is code for the combat sport, of which the king was so passionately fond, a dangerous contest for kings in the best of circumstances. A few decades earlier English King Henry VIII had been knocked unconscious for 20 minutes by a jousting shaft slapped up the side of his head. Hence when he stirred back to consciousness he foreswore ever galloping down the lists again. Regular exercise ended, so began his physical decline and increasing weakness for food binging and self-induced barfing so he could have seconds, thirds, and fourths "add nausea". Henry VIII, by the sunset of his life, cast a far larger and corpulent inflation of his former athletic self, dying of gout and heart failure in 1547.

A commoner might regard how vulgar and inappropriate it was. Nostradamus, that is, publishing a presage throughout the realm of a young lion of a man apparently blinding the French king by two mortal wounds. Is it not so that predicting such a tragedy openly conjures up evil magic daring Satan to make it so?

The man should be put in chains and sent to the Justices of the Church for a good "interrogation" with thumbscrews. Let him "embrace" an iron maiden. Let "her" help puncture a confession out of him. Just what Lutheran heresy was Nostradamus selling?

Ah, but there were other fictions and rumors around court. Those who had a copy of his little book of prophecies would pull it from their sleeve and read—to those who couldn't—a brighter fate for the king. If Henri didn't die in a future tournament, Nostradamus promised he would become a "second Charlemagne." He'd restore peace between

French Protestant Huguenots and the Catholic majority. Even Savoy and Northern Italy would become French under Henri II.

This Nostradamus, so gracious! Trying ever so hard to please everybody, no doubt he pleased the king right out of the audience chamber, satisfied at least by an idea of freedom being his to choose a fate he preferred. Yet, like most men, high or low, Henri chose to forget fate altogether. He lived for the day, for some fresh air, a good horse ride and the fair arms of Diane de Poitiers, his mistress.

Anyway, who can alter fate? It's all God's will, isn't it? I've been told that, just like you, more than once. We believe it too. I'm sure you do, even if it's hidden from your conscious mind, since we were children, highborn or low.

Who can really choose one future over another? Doesn't the Sunday school teacher say it's all preordained? Of course we believe him, because as children we learn it's easier to surrender to authority. Big adult dogma doesn't tolerate or reward child-"light" contrariness.

Four years after Nostradamus had his audience, towards the end of June 1559, Henri II designed to cap off celebrating a festive dual marriage: the first, by proxy, of his daughter Elizabeth de Valois to King Philip II of Spain; the other, in person, his sister Marguerite to the Duke of Savoy. There would be a tournament held along the sawdust-covered Rue de St. Antoine beside the Chateau de Tournelles in the center of Paris where highborn and low could marvel at their virile king resplendent in gilded iron-plated helmet with a golden visor.

On the third day of the tournament, for the final round near sunset, the 41-year-old monarch braced himself for a charge down the lists at his 35-year old Captain of the Scottish Guard, Gabriel de Lorges, the Comte de Montmorency.

In this way, fiction forecasted became fact...

The young lion will overcome the older one,
On the field of combat in single battle...

During an encore charge, one final pass, Montgomery failed to drop his lance in time. A rumor later spread amongst Catholics at court that the Huguenot Montgomery let his sympathies for the "Lutheran" cause keep his lance held high on purpose. Whatever the motivation (or perhaps through mere oversight), a moment later shards of his shattered lance pierced the gilded cage of the king's visor.

> *...He will pierce his eyes through a golden cage:*
> *Two wounds made one, then he dies a cruel death.*

When the bloody gilded helmet was lifted carefully off his head, the surgeons discovered two jagged splinters: one penetrated deep into the king's forehead. A second had pierced his eye socket. He had somehow managed to walk himself to a bedchamber at the Chateau de Tournelles, withdrawing at last from the tumult of the panicked and terrified audience, including Queen Catherine in the royal gallery, who had fainted. Though his eye was intact, it was blinded. The wooden fragment had entered the eye socket, severing the optic nerve before plunging too deep inside his brain for removal. All attempts to pull it out produced such agonized cries from the king that this diagnosis was the only thing the surgeon could draw.

No longer in his armor or fussed over by his physicians, the king called in musicians. They played light music and he waited. The marriage would go on without him. The citizens of Paris began their watch. Had two wounds made one regicide?

You can't call anyone writing about the future a "non-fiction" author, even though publishers stick that label on you. What really is "non-fictional" about witnessing visions of things that haven't happened? If free will changes the future, your "non-fiction" might never happen. Indeed, one might want to write books of future fantasy that somehow never come true. Your credibility as a seer is happily sacrificed if, in some way, a book you write about tomorrow's most dire potentials never happens because your writing had some impact in changing the future. Thus you are "rewarded" by being called "liar" at worst; or, you become just a fool to forget.

Who cares what they think.

The true reward you secretly hold in your heart is that your dire fiction about the future remained a fiction because you helped people change the future.

One day I carried quince apples up a quiet country road on the edge of my island village in anticipation of planting myself before the rickety fence to wave and whistle before the field of stampeding sheep catching sight of my hand-held apples. Rather than a phalanx of lumbering wool advancing up the hilly field in my direction, it was empty of ungulates. In place of them there *stood*, without standing, a *ball doorway*. Latchless and ajar.

Imagination had burned like a fuel propelling it there on the field having become a background to the inner reverie of my mind, all at once, like electric connections making a spark by light of thought. When this sphere doorway expands, it touches and absorbs—it *becomes*—instantly what it contacts. All it touched *inside* the shrinking infinite, it also "became."

Sight embraced everything touched upon!

The sphere-door grew outward. Its surface was like an eyeball-shaped *seeing*, all around, orbed observation rather than directional.

"I" was the cathode light of thought that "opened" this "eye."

Weird?

Try this one on…

Once upon another life, in another space-time, a man was walking out from under a spread of pine trees, beyond the bending bowers, his weathered face now warmed by the Sun, trekking with staff in hand and cows in attendance. He didn't have apples to feed sheep. He was a cowherd leading his ungulates of hoof and moos into a broad, grassy clearing.

The time must have been the 1770s.

Difficult to say.

The man didn't have a watch. Couldn't read, either. This illiterate cowherd—some say his name was Mattias Lang, others record his name as Mattias Stormberger... Anyway, he was hiking through the forest on any one of countless times during his regulated adult life, leading his cows out from under the pine-needle eaves, bestride the picturesque villages of Kalteneck and Deggendorf to graze on fields close to the border of Bavaria with Bohemia. One day he must have seen that "iron road" in his field, perhaps in the same way I witnessed the "Sphere Door" in mine.

If celestial spheres exist, and if they sing the prophetic electric of potential, echoing in future times our present actions in harmonic or discordant karmic consequence, then they are the globe-shaped advent inside a seer made a vehicle of multi-universal possibilities.

The concept of mad augury is no longer out of range of rational possibility. The melancholia of divinatory trance has a friend in measurable Quantum Theory. Consider when watching one of two quantum particles, each in different locales. It has been scientifically proven that the observation of one of these particles in one place immediately changes the other.

Your life lived in the present, each moment, changes another place, called the future.

The witness of present and future is *Consciousness.*

Some say consciousness is neither the present nor the future, yet its awareness of present and future changes them in this dimension called "Present" and in a parallel dimension of "Future."

Consciousness at the center of Existence is a fundamental idea of a new and revolutionary scientific theory called Biocentrism. It has among its adherents Dr. Robert Lanza, who the *New York Times* voted third most important scientist alive.

In his book entitled "*Biocentrism: How Life and Consciousness Are the Keys to Understanding the Nature of the Universe,*" Lanza theorizes that science may have the concept of consciousness all upside down. The popular scientific theory defines consciousness as being solely an illusion of some electro-chemical phenomenon of the brain. When your gray matter ceases to function at the body and brain's death, *poof* goes your consciousness. Lanza proposes, along with a growing number of fellow scientists, physicists and astrophysicists that consciousness abides in parallel worlds in a great continuum of multiverses.

Consciousness may not be a product of your body-mind but the sentient driver of your corporeal vehicle in life. If your embodied reality should run its natural course and die out, are you as dead as your old car? If the radio cannot receive "your" consciousness signal, does that mean there's no signal? Oh, the sentient radio wave was just an illusion spooked up by the old radio before the fuses burned out.

I have long meditated on a counterintuitive concept establishing *Chaos* as the mother of all vehicles of consciousness, such as this particular Universe we inhabit and all things in it. Purpose and plan is born of accident and happenstance. With time, accident brings on evolutionary changes. The "vehicles" such as primates and hominids become sophisticated vectors or mediums to "pick up" the signal of eternal consciousness. Sentient "soul" abides in flesh to express itself in the mortal universe through us.

Subjective prophecy found its Science Fiction respectability in the person, H.G. Wells, who, two years prior to Morgan Robertson laboring on his Titanic-"Titan" tale, wrote *The Door in the Wall* in 1895, the first story ever submitted about unique, inter-dimensional worlds existing simultaneously like quark particles.

In an article entitled *Scientists Claim that Quantum Theory Proves Consciousness Moves to Another Universe At Death* (Psychology, 12 January 2014) Dr. Hugh Everett took up Wells' idea for his thesis at Princeton University:

> *It basically posits that at any given moment the universe divides into countless similar instances. And the next moment, these "newborn" universes split in a similar fashion. In some of these worlds you may be present: reading this article in one universe, or watching TV in another.*
>
> *The triggering factor for these multiplying worlds is our actions... If we make some choices, instantly one universe splits into two with different versions of outcomes.*

Astrological prophecy proposes that we have entered a new 2,000-year epoch. The Aquarian Age promises science will at last take us, for better or worse, beyond the faith-based epoch of the Piscean Age. Inventions will remove the barriers belief had built between the objective and subjective worlds—between so-called life and so-called death. The process of invention starts right now as progressive scientists come forth positing new ways of thinking about old laws of physics and metaphysics. The visions of prophets of a time continuum where all past-present-future events in multiple timelines running through multiple universes that exist simultaneously are not psychotic episodes. They will soon be scientifically explained. The existence of soul will be proven in no less a fundamental way than radio waves had been measured. It only takes the evolution of the "receiving" body-mind "radio" to advance its mind and sensitivity, pushing the limits of theory and experimentation. Physicists like Andrei Linde of the Lebedev's Institute of Physics at Stanford University had already stepped beyond theoretical comfort zones to explain the following in the early 1980s:

> *Space consists of many inflating spheres, which give rise to similar spheres, and those, in turn, produce spheres in even greater numbers, and so on to infinity. In the universe, they are spaced apart. They are not aware of each other's existence. But they represent parts of the same physical universe.*

The spherical door in my field of sheep is such a thing. I believe the same had "opened" without opening inside Stormberger's inner sight. One dimension observed instantly changed the other without them touching. *Visioned* by Stormberger was a road of iron. It was there in the field in one "fourth" dimension of time inside his mind, sparking an image through a bundle of brain nerves receiving a twentieth-century signal; and, it was simultaneously *not there* in the other fourth dimension timeline running the reality of a farming field in the eighteenth-century.

Dr. Stuart Hamaroff and British physicist Sir Roger Penrose theorize that consciousness touches our "receiver" of the body mind using the microtubules of the brain cells, which he thinks are the primary sites of quantum processing. In this manner, three billion years of chaos-birthed evolution had paradoxically ordered itself to create at last a sentient receptor fashioned out of matter that picks up the signal of the "matterless" consciousness existing and witnessing multiple universes of multiple quantum timeliness and histories. It can create prophets and visionaries out of us all, if we could just relax and allow openness to settle into *this* eternity in a dewdrop of *moment*.

I believe Stormberger's inner eye *saw* what was inside his mind projected upon the outside. An iron horse in a fourth-dimensional reality passing where he stood on the field in the temporal dimension he physically occupied that had become a screen for microtubules caressing nerve clusters inside his mind the image of the train from another time.

This is all fiction, of course.

What Stormberger and I have seen of the future is a fiction in "our" timeline. It is no less fictional than sinking Titans, and kings embracing a replay of Charlemagne's glory or getting their eye pierced and life snuffed out in a joust.

I have not invented this pure fiction. Nevertheless, our actions make time travelers and time-alterers out of us all. A fiction "can" be true but not made manifest unless our actions invite fictional potentials in *The Future* to manifest in this *Present*.

Lamentations echoed through the halls and lay prostrate in the bedchambers of the Chateau de Tournelles. The queen was inconsolable and catatonic with grief. Courtiers and ladies-in-waiting carried her away.

The king is dead…

Two wounds made one life end with an infection festering upon the unremoved splinter in a brain that doctors of that unhygienic time had no power to cure. The fever had slowly drained life out of Henri II. He died the cruel, hard death foreseen, lingering for ten days after his jousting accident. If there was an alternative reality where he reigned as Second Charlemagne to unite French Catholic and Protestant and prevent a series of religious civil wars from bleeding France, it was a dream without a planet or a king to make it so for anyone left behind on a timeline burning down the candle of a night death watch in early July 1559.

De Lorges, Comte de Montgomery, the younger man who had accidentally killed him, the Captain of Henri's Scottish Guard, the bearer of the second lion's shield in a field of combat on the Rue de St. Antoine, felt stabbed by grief upon hearing the bells toll the dirge. He cried out in protest, "Cursed be the divine who predicted it, so evilly and so well!"

Why is it, that bearers of warnings of futures to be avoided are cursed and not the act of the recipient's unheeding? If I warn you of a danger approaching, why do you judge the visionary as a harbinger of evil if evil is allowed to happen because of your willful ignorance of making the right choices? Rather, should we not curse our denial of oncoming and clearly foretold danger in the bitter aftermath of hindsight? Henri had been warned twice by two noted seers about something any educated guess weighing the chances, free of the hectoring of soothsayers, should have been enough to conclude that the odds for future safety were long.

Participating in life-and-limb threatening tournaments at age 41?

You and I in the twenty-first century might think 50 is the new 40 but hard living in the sixteenth-century on average marked 40 as the *old* 60. Henri, though certainly youthful for his age, had tempted fate and stretched his athletic passion deep enough into midlife to hang up his jousting stick, clamp closed forever his golden-visor and put away his armor for the sake of the realm. What else was the "divine" spark of prophecy using Nostradamus for, if common sense wasn't enough?

It is, at least, noble of Henri II that during his terrible final ten days he didn't protest his fate. He accepted it, perhaps with the certitude of a mediocre king. Mediocrities find it easy to be certain without too much reflection or perspective. He felt more comfortable charging up and down the lists like a wild lion first, ruling like a king, second.

Thus he found himself rendered into a piece of carrion by a sudden, realm-undermining, nation-destabilizing accident that no responsible, middle aged and maturing man would risk, especially when his sons were too young to rule, and religious civil war was afoot.

No successful prophet goes unpunished.

On the night when news of the king's death had reached the streets of Paris carried by the doleful sounding of church bells, a rabble in a rank mood pushed through a downcast throng gathering and praying before the offices of the Justices of the Church. They carried aloft in torchlight the body of the prophet Nostradamus impaled on a stake. They set their torches on the scarecrow scryer fabricated out of canvas, straw and costumed in a hand-me-down, three-cornered scholar's cap and threadbare robes. The agents of the Roman Inquisition had gathered at the threshold to watch the mob burn Nostradamus. They also heard the people demand immolation in earnest of the evil one's flesh and bones, who by predicting the king's death must have had some Satanic part in making it so.

As luck would have it, Nostradamus was hundreds of miles to the south of Paris, a full, two-month-long horse or oxen cart ride from the capital, in sunny, sleepy Provence.

He had left Paris in the middle of the night four years before in the summer of 1555, after drawing horoscopes for Queen Catherine's sons. A woman he described as having great beauty and noble bearing tipped him off. It was time to get out of town. The Church Justices wished to interrogate him concerning his magical and astrological practices.

His prophecy of the joust failed to save a king, yet it made Nostradamus immortal. He lives on as myth and medium, a king of prophets, the controversy still alive. His cryptic and often nebulous prophecies perpetuate lively discussion and debate even now, nearly four-and-a-half centuries after his peaceful passing in 1566. The Inquisition's rack never bit. No fire melted his flesh because while he lived, the widowed Queen Catherine de Medici, his disciple and protector, became Queen Regent, de facto ruler of France.

Mattias Stormberger, an unschooled peasant cowherd of Bavaria, was born around 1756. He was that rare prophet who, before dying circa 1820, found someone to document and publish his oral predictions. Some of these reflections survived the book burnings of Nazis in the 1930s. Among them was his most famous forecast:

Iron roads will be built, and iron monsters will bark through the wilderness. Cars without horse and shaft will come, and men will fly through the air like birds...

Stormberger as a simple peasant tending his cows had seen the "fictions" above perhaps as early as his twenties back in the 1770s. The inventions of automobiles and airplanes along with trains on their iron tracks, imposed themselves in visions projected on his peaceful, bucolic forest, skies and sunny fields of a pre-industrial Bavarian countryside.

Here recounts further the surviving singed fragments of Stormberger's tale of prophecy:

...When on the outskirts of the forest, the iron road will be finished, and there the iron horse will be seen, a war will begin, to last for twice two years. It will be fought with iron fortresses that move without horses, and with powers that come from the earth and fall from the sky.

His reverie of battle tanks became the future's reality. They were first invented and used in a war that "did" last four years. The war began EXACTLY on the day a rail line running alongside Stormberger's Bavarian forest between Kalteneck and Deggendorf was opened for rolling stock with great pomp and waving of the red, white and black tricolors of Imperial Germany.

The "powers" of warfare's future weapons Stormberger saw and heard screaming out "from the sky" were the artillery shells for guns of August 1914, in the opening salvoes of the First World War. Germany's entry began on 1 August, the day the rail line between Kalteneck and Deggendorf had opened!

The "powers of the earth" would shovel out the vast labyrinth trench networks of the Western Front. He describes weapons in the earth, the great mines planted by miners digging tunnels under enemy trench lines, letting issue after great detonations and geysers of falling mud, a rush and tumble of soldiers, pouring over a lunar landscape of barbed wire and horrors, advancing, closer, closer, towards waiting death's finger pressing on rifle and machine-gun trigger.

Many would die, often murdered by another foreseen power "from the air": mustard and chlorine gas exploding out of artillery air blasts—a fiction that became fact as well in the four years of World War One (1914-1918).

Stormberger? Too much of your fiction finds fact!

By the 1930s, accurate forecasts about the war's length and weapons used in the First World War were enough to motivate the Gestapo, Hitler's secret police, to confiscate his writings and throw books and pamphlets on flaming pyres with other books written by soothsayers, degenerates—Jews. Accurate prophecy was again "rewarded," this time with immolation. The Nazis wanted to render the future's potential facts into crinkling ash-flaked fictions by purging them with fire. They didn't want Germans to know what Stormberger might prophesy about Hitler's future war plans.

Stormberger and Nostradamus are the most prominent of a small group of seers one can define as "World War Prophets." Looking back with hindsight at their documented predictions they all share an undeniable accuracy presaging dates and details about the First and Second World Wars often centuries before these tragedies took place.

For instance, Nostradamus wrote in these two verses about the First World War and what evil it would birth, the Russian "Red" communist revolution:

2 Q1
Toward Aquitaine [France] *the British make assaults,*
They make great incursions:
Rains and frosts make the terrain unsafe and uneven,
Against the port of those of the Crescent [The Turks]
they will make mighty invasions.

The "Great War" as it was also called inspired this prophecy of vast battles stretching across thousands of miles with armies as numerous as the whole population of a country in Nostradamus' own day. Gone are the baggy-sleeved pikemen and glittering knights. All illusions of chivalry are lost in a nightmare vision of the Western Front he's trying to describe. Future soldiers cower and die like rats in a soggy, uneven, shell-blasted wasteland of barbed wire and swollen corpses. In the next line, he takes us a thousand miles east to the approaches of Istanbul where men scale the steep, sunbaked cliffs of the Dardanelles to fall before rasping Turkish machine-guns.

8 Q80

Blood of the innocent, of the widow and virgin,
So many evils committed by means of the Great Red.
Holy Icons placed over burning candles.
Terrified by fear, none will be seen to move.

The Bolshevik government of Vladimir Lenin (nicknamed the "Great Red" prince of terror) ordered thousands of Russian Orthodox churches systematically dynamited and countless religious icons burned. After Lenin arose an even greater Red beast, Joseph Stalin, whose reign of terror over his own subjects was the greatest of the twentieth century. Stalin liquidated at least 10 million Soviets and an equal number disappeared or died in Siberian labor camps. The prophecy's first line can be applied to the vicious execution of the last Czarina and her virgin daughters, or it is a general description of those numberless victims of Stalinism.

Our times are eerily beginning to match the blithe-and-blind march of idiot Western shepherd leaders and their herds of *sheeple*, to the slaughtering fields of a new world war in *2014*. Moreover, the world war prophets—Nostradamus, Stormberger and others presented in this book—share a vision of not two, but THREE world wars happening.

Here we are, 22 years-and-counting from the end of the Cold War. The forgetfulness in a generation's passing rivals that of 1914. I hear and see today's European Union and American politicians precipitously pushing around the Russian Federation as if it's another little country like puny Iraq or Libya, ripe for regime change. Russia, however, is a *nuclear power*—it really *does* have weapons of mass destruction. What madness has gotten into politicians in Washington when they dare even countenance backing to the wall a nation, a world power, like Russia when it possesses nearly 4,484 immediately deliverable nuclear warheads out of a total stockpile of 8,500?

Ever since the cold war ended, Moscow has watched agreements broken and marked a steady encroachment and the conversion to NATO of countries on Russia's European frontiers. Washington seems nostalgic, or "nuke-stalgic," backwards looking, caught under the spell of a new kind of war hawk fever.

This time it's a rare, bipartisan condition.

Neoconservatives from the Republican right and American Exceptionalists from the Democrat left began philosophically converging ever since the end of the Cold War in 1989 and by the mid 2010s seem close to creating a reality to match their false projections of a new Russian threat requiring a new cold war to contain it.

Russian Federation president, Vladimir Putin, doesn't scare me half as much as leaders in Washington, such as President Obama, and those technocrats presiding over the European Union in Brussels ganging up on him. Prophecies in this book will show Obama and other Western heads of state are grasping a glass for a long, deep gulp of the collective "kook-aid" in 2014, like Western leaders did in 1914. Both, one century apart, run an over-militarized world that any military miscalculation could push brinksmanship beyond the best laid and shortsighted plans projected on new and uncertain times.

Currently there are less conventional options to fighting wars. The steps of escalation are far fewer. A tempting and rapid rush to fire unconventional chemical, biological and nuclear weapons, is far more likely.

The atomic and thermonuclear weapon inventory of 2014 reports that NATO's infernal war chest consists of America's 7,506, plus France's 300 and the United Kingdom's 250 warheads, adds up to a grand total of 8,031 warheads pointed at the Russian Federation's total of 8,484 warheads. Thankfully, it's not the 45,000 Soviet and 32,000 US warheads on a hair trigger at the peak of the last cold war. Moreover, the Center of Arms Control and Non-Proliferation report the strategic and non-strategic deployed and war-ready weapons in NATO's doomsday quiver number 2,372 against Russia's 4,684.

Do not let that assuage your illusions like it does leaders in Washington and Brussels. It is enough nuclear Armageddon *bang* to kill your civilization and if Nostradamus and other seers behold the future dangers right, it's enough to kill off two-thirds of the human race!

It is frightening to fathom just where this gathering blindness in leadership will lead the blind world next.

History doesn't repeat itself. Stupidity does.

Sometimes a radical agent must expose it. Sometimes one has to look ahead, look into the future, aided by the greatest seers with clear forecasts and documented success at anticipating our next stupid steps before we march blind-eyed, bushy tailed like they did back in 1914 knuckle-headlong into a civilization changing—or this time "ending"—catastrophe.

Will 2014 be the same as 1914?

Are we that stupid again?

This book sounds a prophetic alarm so that some future fictions remain forever fictional. We will examine how Stormberger, like Nostradamus, and other seers would repeat their successful and detailed auguries down to the dating of not one or two but "three" world wars. Of the third, Stormberger said, "With open eyes will the people of the Earth enter into these catastrophes."

This book aims to enlighten you to the clear and present danger of nuclear war "and" help you "open eyes" in time to SEE the danger, thus preventing this future from happening.

chapter one

Cold War One
And the Brothers of the North

I am a child born of the last Cold War. I was an atomic bomb baby, as astrologers would define those of us celebrating our birthdays under Pluto in fiery Leo (1939-1957), especially those of us pinned into our first diapers in the last two-thirds of Pluto's transit when the US and Soviet Union regularly lit off atmospheric atomic and thermonuclear hydrogen bomb tests. Indeed, the mid-to-late 1950s were the peak years for above-ground testing. Along with lesser nuclear powers, Britain, France and later China, the nuclear powers practiced nuclear war on tropical islands, Soviet steppes and US desert lands of indigenous nations of the Fourth World. In this phony war the planet's air and ecology were also targeted by 2,053 atomic (fission) and thermonuclear (fusion) bombs of all megaton calibers. Untold thousands of humans living downwind of radioactive fallout clouds have already died of cancer from testing doomsday until the US and USSR signed the Partial Nuclear Test Ban Treaty ending atmospheric detonations on 10 October 1963 after lighting off 528 above ground and ocean blasts. Thousands more underground tests would continue uninterrupted for another 33 years, razing evacuated tropical atolls below sea level and collapsing sink holes in Nevada, Central Asia, and the Indian Rajasthan desert. Other mountain tests in Pakistan and North Korea caused major rockslides, all of which can often leak radiation. Mock-doomsday rehearsals finally ended with the signing of the Comprehensive Test Ban Treaty in 1996.

Every day of the Cold War, every moment of life lived in all its light and dark moments had the point of a sword of Damocles shaped like a missile-tipped nuclear threat hanging over every living thing. In the back of nearly everyone's mind was a fear that at any moment, by some accident or intent, stars manufactured by science and handed over to intolerant, politically righteous, unpeaceful men could devour by fire our whole world. Life or death hung on one of these political creatures pressing a button, sending tens of thousands of Intercontinental Ballistic Missiles (ICBMs) aloft. After a 30-minute rocket ride through space, the warheads would re-enter the atmosphere, to blossom hell fire over tens of thousands of cities and military targets. The light of death in manmade flaming stars would begin the scorching of Earth around southernmost targets and then advance a doomsday barrage northwards across the United States, Europe and the Soviet Union.

We children of the atom bomb threat used to have nightmares about ourselves and all whom we loved skeletonized by nuclear heat blasts; or, if not directly hit, with hair and nails falling out, we dreamed of succumbing to the terrible agonies of radiation sickness. If one was lucky enough to avoid both, a phantasm about famine was waiting to strangle our stomachs, shocking us to awaken. The back note in my life of that traumatic thought, was brought first to my tender mind when, just days before my eighth birthday, the Cuban Missile Crisis happened—the closest the world came to a cold war going suddenly hot, only resolving itself at the 11th hour.

Picture the unthinkable alternative future. The US Navy and Air Force unleash full-scale air attacks on Soviet missiles based in Cuban jungles and US forces hit the Cuban beaches. These are atomized by the tactical nuclear weapons that mere Soviet battalion commanders can access on an active battlefield without permission from Moscow's centralized military command. Shortly after, American manufactured stars would devour Cuba, but not before most of the missiles the Soviets had secretly stationed there, just 99 miles off the US coast would have launched. Five minutes later, Los Angeles along with 30 cities and 20 million people would have become blazing victims from what Hopi

Native American prophets had warned was the white man's "Gourd of Ashes."

A Hopi gourd stood on its neck is shaped like a mushroom cloud. Nostradamus tried to describe the same cloud as "a stone in the tree"— a cooling ball of superheated gas and debris of a nuclear blast rising many miles into the air on a pillar of ash after it cremated a city.

Terrible are the images these words share today, yet for me they are no longer filled with pain and fear. I hold onto them as a simple, factual remembrance ever since Christmas Day 1991, when the communist Soviet Union lost its long and mostly political-economic battle with the US and the so-called "free world." The sword of Damocles had been taken down and put back in its missile silo sheath. We all had awakened from the Cold War and its nightmares were over. The Soviet hegemon simply unraveled with its military alliance, the Warsaw Pact of Eastern European satellites, disbanding and sloughing off their communist governments. The hammer-and-sickle flag was lowered off the Kremlin flagpole for the last time after dusk on Christmas Day 1991. Up went the old imperial tricolor of pre-communist, czarist-Russian past. Later, the golden double-headed czarist eagle emblem was rehabilitated to its former place on flags displayed during state functions, centered and spreading its wings from the tricolor's central blue field. The standard of the czars now passes on to become the standard of the Russian Federation's president.

The Soviet Union became the Russian Federation surrounded by breakaway Soviet Socialist Republics like the Baltic mini nations of Lithuania, Latvia and Estonia. The flagpoles of half-a-dozen new "Stans" of the former Central Asian Soviet Republics hoisted their new ensigns of independence. There emerged the new states of Belarus, Georgia, and Ukraine with a new "toe" of a peninsula, the very un-Ukrainian Russian province the Ukrainian born Premier Nikita Khrushchev had added to his homeland in 1954. He, like other Russian leaders, had merged a number of predominantly Russian populated provinces to the eastern end of Ukraine for mostly bureaucratic reasons.

As early as 1992, future watchers like myself considered predominantly Russian Crimea's incorporation into Ukraine a future flashpoint for war. What if Kiev didn't renew or suspended Moscow's lease to use its strategic naval base at Sevastopol and the Black Sea Fleet? What would Russia do if its only harbor access to temperate oceans were threatened with closure? Time would tell.

Prophecy watchers under the spell of a cold-war mindset, colored their conclusions according more to the expectations of the times than what prophets actually might have meant with their "stones in trees" and other metaphorical "out of their Gourd of Ashes" riddles. What else could the Cold War be but a prelude to a final, biblical battle of Armageddon? The era's interpreters of prophecy sought and often found what their deepest fears were looking for at the unconscious exclusion of all other possible scenarios. Armageddon was a nuclear war pitting Russia against America over Arab-Israeli conflicts and who would control the so-called Holy Land and the oil underneath. The two had already fought several conventional wars in the Middle East through proxies. We prophecy scholars got it mostly and fortunately wrong when the Cold War died with a whimper rather than a bang in 1989, even though I published the possibility of it ending quietly with the 1980s because of something I'd seen in Nostradamus' prophecies five years before.

Adolf Hitler was reasonably confident even before the Cold War began that it wouldn't come to doomsday blows. On the eve of the Battle of Berlin, Hitler had descended underground to live his final days in the tomblike quarters of his Fuehrer bunker, underneath the German capital. On 2 April 1945, he contemplated the unthinkable: life after *Der Untergang* (the downfall) of the Third Reich in total defeat. Not more than a fortnight later, German Army regulars and fanatic SS troopers would make their last stand against a Soviet jugger-naut rolling and thundering out the East above his stooped head and shoulders. Hitler's secretary Martin Bormann set down for posterity one of his master's final spoken prophecies. It was as if Hitler could already hear the approaching battle shaking the bunker's cement ceiling when he dictated the following:

With the defeat of the Reich and pending the emergence of the Asiatic, the African, and perhaps the South American nationalisms, there will remain in the world only two great powers capable of confronting each other—the United States and Soviet Russia. The laws of both history and geography will compel these two powers to a trial of strength, either military or in the fields of economics or ideology. And it is equally certain that both these powers will sooner or later find it desirable to seek the support of the sole surviving great nation in Europe, the German people.

Evil can sometimes perceive the future clearer because evil instinctively, intuitively exploits the latent, serial predictability of our darker habits and human weaknesses. These habitual blind spots of unconsciousness are behind what makes our future so predictable. Hence a man like Hitler foresaw the oncoming era of postcolonial revolutions in Africa and South America. He had anticipated the post-war breakup of the British Empire in observations recorded early in the war, when he was winning. Hitler had said, "In this war, in the event of [allied] victory, only America will gain an advantage. In the event of [our] defeat, it's England who will be only the loser." (1942)

Hitler's Cold War prophecy uttered less than a month before he put a bullet through his head, sagely predicted the next world war that was waged primarily with weapons of ideology and economics. Note how he gives more emphasis to these as his final thought in the sentence: *The laws of both history and geography will compel these two powers to a trial of strength, either military or in the fields of economics or ideology.*

The USSR lost that trial of strength politically and economically with the United States. It folded up its Warsaw Pact, disbanded its armies, put lock and key on its nuclear stockpile. Moscow began dismantling its nuclear arsenal in stages for two succeeding decades, as did Washington, both fulfilling their obligations to START (the Strategic Arms Reduction Treaty).

Moscow and Washington's cold war arsenal of civilization-ending atomic and thermonuclear weapons kept the two nuclear colossi from gambling on a direct conventional military trial of strength. Both anticipated the main battlefield would be across divided Germany where 40,000 Soviet and Warsaw Pact tanks had a long-odds chance of charging rapidly into West Germany's Fulda Gap, deep enough into

Western Europe, defeating NATO conventional forces, before their commanders ordered up battlefield nuclear weapons or intercontinental missiles.

The ultimate standoff called MAD (Mutually Assured Destruction) sustained a perverted peace by the sheer-terror weaponry both sides had stockpiled. It worked like this: push the proverbial button of a doomsday missile launch in a first strike and the other side still has enough time in 30 minutes remaining to lift off a full, retaliatory response. Both combatant superpowers are thus mutually destroyed in less than an hour. Moreover, the Soviet communists, being citizens of an officially atheist nation, don't believe in God, Heaven or an Afterlife. They want to keep here "here" in one piece as long as they and theirs will live. The Soviets kept their missiles in their silos in a defensive stance for the entire Cold War, despite the US propaganda characterizing "godless" commies always on the ready to stealthily launch an auto-suicidal first strike. When a communist believes God is not only *not* on your side but doesn't exist, he or she might love staying alive more than the God-and-Heaven believers do in America, the land the Bible built. Heaven's a dangerous belief when one puts faith in a conceit that God loves one and Heaven waits for one even after one blows up the world.

The Cold War I lived through witnessed Washington and Moscow handle several potential nuclear crises with surprising discipline and temperance. Luck and enough rational leaders as earnest watchmen on both sides helped humanity soldier through those few world-terrifying moments when strategic miscalculations like the Cuban Missile Crisis, and potentially "crossing the red line" threats, such as the 1967 Six Day War and Yom Kippur War (1973), rubbed the mutually assured standoff raw. Only once did a Soviet Premier openly debate moving Soviet nuclear forces from a defensive to offensive stance. President Ronald Reagan's "Evil Empire" speech in 1983 convinced Premier Andropov that God-loving and Heaven-after-death believing Ronnie had gone either insane or senile. He had the KGB reports in hand confirming Reagan heeded the holy-rolling counsel of evangelical American preachers who kept feeding into his head their Sunday school doomsday take on biblical prophecy. Armageddon was near and it would blaze from an imminent nuclear war with Russia.

Reagan went to press about it; he openly confided to a *Wall Street Journal* reporter. "I don't know whether you know, but a great many theologians over a number of years…have been struck by the fact that in recent years, as in no other time in history, most of these prophecies have been coming together."

Andropov thought such comments proved Reagan believed he was the US president of biblical end times. Would he therefore make doomsday happen accidentally on portentous purpose?

We can thank Andropov's chief advisor—the future and final Soviet Premier Mikhail Gorbachev—for calming him down. Reagan was just nuclear terror trash talking to his political base counseled Gorbachev, he didn't really intend to blow up the USSR.

The world war prophets knew we would survive all the dangers of the Cold War. Eastern Mediterranean seers identified as Sibylline Oracles, their lineage starting as far back as the second-century B.C.E., are among the earliest members of this prescient club. Greek and Roman legend define a *Sibyl* as a woman imbued with oracular insight by the god Apollo. The lineage of Sibylline Oracles took up the early Christian faith, the last being a third-century C.E. prophetess from Babylon. Her surviving verses contain accurate predictions concerning the spread of Christianity as well as prophecies anticipating the Apocalypse.

Move forward in time to the Middle Ages. Meet St. Odile, living in the eighth century. She was patroness of Alsace, France and Abbess of Hohenburg (Odilienberg) Monastery in the Vosges Mountains. She was born totally blind. Her father, Adalric of Alsace, believed it an evil omen and had the child banished to a nunnery. Her intense devotion to God was already apparent even at such a tender age. So was her ability to predict the future, which she said came as a result of learning how to live without sight. It is claimed her vision was miraculously restored by the intensity of her prayers and the healing powers of the local bishop. Her father heard of this and reconsidered bringing her out of the convent to marry her off. He ordered her brought home yet she soon found the lifestyle of a pampered princess unappealing and persuaded her father to convert one of his castles into a nunnery, where she lived out her days as its abbess. St. Odile's prophecies are said to be her final written testament before dying in 720.

Except for the Babylonian Sibyl and Nostradamus, a Frenchman from Provence, the rest of the club of world war augurs are ethnic Germans. Along with St. Odile and Stormberger there's the thirteenth-century Austrian monk named Johann Friede (1204-1257). Little else about him survives except for one prophecy. Next is Pastor Bartholomaeus Holzhauser of Swabia (1612-1658). He was a professor of theology and pastor of St. Johann Church in the Tyrol (Austria). At the age of 14, he was already respected for his insights into religious matters. Often praying in seclusion, zealous and strict in his fasts and religious ardor, the peasant folk of his congregation revered him as a model holy man. Princes and kings praised him for the depth of his intellect. He was often a guest in the court of Johann Philipp, Elector of Mayence.

Is the German majority a coincidence?

Is a karmic resonance at play here?

All four German seers of vastly different times equally loved peace. Like Nostradamus, their surviving written prophecies belie a predilection for a kind of quantitative viewing of the future, only in reverse. There are two dimensions of time and each holds a quantum "particle". One particle is a German seer in the past dimension, the other particle is a German living in a future dimension. What the German in the future sees simultaneously "changes" the German in the past who has the gift of prophecy to "see the future German's experience."

Quantum Prophecy Theory, if you like, believes that consciousness can expand to a higher awareness beyond the limits of temporal reality to view a great Continuum. The so-called past, present and future time lines are no longer experienced as either separate or linear but exist all at once.

The "change" the German in the past experiences from the seeing and experiencing of the German in the future dimension is a glimpse of that higher consciousness of *Evernow*, if you will, the great simultaneous reality, yet it is expressed by the German prophet in the past dimension as a prophecy.

I believe the past German seers in the world war prophecy club were charmed by the future to prophesy what German people in the future had unleashed: the First and Second World Wars.

Even Hitler foresaw Germany's special role in the Cold War that followed:

And it is equally certain that both these powers [America and Russia] *will sooner or later find it desirable to seek the support of the sole surviving great nation in Europe, the German people.*

It was true. The active help of West and East Germans was sought. They lived divided by the Iron Curtain's uncrossed red line of barbed-wired border and Berlin-walled division at its most tense checkpoint. The Cold War ended in 1989 because the Germans tore down the Berlin Wall.

Stormberger dated and described Germany in the First World War. Next he related to his scribe, perhaps at the time of his death around 1820, events in post-World-War One Germany, a century before they happened, when his people would be blamed for a war that many historians still argue was the mistake of all European combatant governments because they diplomatically entrapped themselves in trip-wire treaties and arms races. Yet the Treaty of Versailles forced Germany to serve as the scapegoat, made to pay reparations causing in part its economy's historic hyperinflation, or, as Stormberger described it:

Right after the horrible war there will come a time when money will have no value. For two hundred guilders, not even a loaf of bread will be available, and yet there will be no famine. Money would be made of iron, and gold will become so valuable that for a few gold coins a small farm could be bought.

There was hunger, certainly, but no sweeping famine across Germany. Nevertheless, at one point in this most terrible of economic depressions of the twentieth century, you would need a suitcase full of two billion Reichmarks to buy a loaf of bread! The German government was hard pressed to print paper money more valuable for barter than wallpaper. They even minted coins out of iron and aluminum.

Apparently, the 1919 Versailles Treaty's draconian "Carthaginian Peace" wasn't harsh enough for chauvinist French Field Marshal Ferdinand Foch. He remarked, "This wasn't a treaty, it is only an armistice of twenty years!"

He had inadvertently forecast a Second World War thundering into view in the year 1939—so apparently did Stormberger whose oral forecasts were published around 1820, a full 99 years before Foch:

Two or three decades after the first great war will come a second, still greater war.

The Versailles Treaty had created a climate of social and economic distress in Germany. The red flag-waving communists on the far left, and swastika-waving National Socialists on the far right, marched and brawled in lawless city streets. The latter won the struggle placing their leader, Adolf Hitler, in power by early 1933. He launched the Second World War in 1939, exactly 20 years after the treaty had been signed in 1919.

Pastor Bartholomaeus viewing life in Germany between the First and Second World War from an oracular vantage point over a century before Stormberger was born, takes up the future tale:

In the second period will be peace, but only by name, not in reality. The tribulations will be as great as during a war. The new rulers of Germany will stand up against authorities. God will pour out the spirit of deception over them, and they will want what they don't want, will not want what they do want, and their actions will become so preposterous, that they will not be able to do what they are able to do. At noonday they will grope about like in darkness.

Germany's descent into a fascist darkness, dressed in the black of SS troops and the Gestapo's secret police state, took place in a *second period of peace* (1919-1939). The first, therefore, would have begun at the end of the Franco-Prussian War in 1871. It lasted 43 years until ending abruptly in August 1914 with the First World War.

The new rulers, Hitler and his Nazi henchmen, once invited to form a coalition government with Hitler as Chancellor, very quickly exploited the act of a single terrorist—a lone communist simpleton to be exact—who set on fire the German Reichstag (Parliament) building. Whether Marinus van der Lubbe was an arsonist or Nazi patsy in a false flag terrorist attack, Hitler grabbed an opportunity that was handed to him freely by a nation in shock. He demanded and received from Parliament "temporary" enabling acts nullifying all checks and balances to his power written in the German constitution until the emergency ended. The new police state arrested all members of the German Communist Party (and branded as terrorists a whole lot of other political adversaries, journalists, promoters of free speech and democracy that dared protest Hitler's new authority). In a few months' time, Hitler had usurped all power to himself, disbanded all trade unions and political parties, except his National Socialist Party and became simply "the Leader" (Der Fuehrer) of Germany. Dictatorship descended on the German people. Hitler's propaganda ministry wove its lies, its false conspiracy theories blaming the Great War capitulation, the economic crashes, the disorder, all on some unproven, irrational Hebrew-phobia and the people began to believe it.

Hitler brought German workers back into full employment and was worshipped like a God presiding over the massive pageants of Nazi rallies. These epic demonstrations of National Socialism bathed so often in bright sunlight on cloudless days inspired many to believe, half in jest, that the Fuehrer could command the skies to cast off the frequently overcast, cold and rainy German climate with what they called "Hitler weather."

Although the Sun at noontime blazed bright, Bartholomaeus perceived the hearts and minds of Germans settling under a deepening spell of dark magic. They would soon follow their dictator into a hell he, and they, created: a Second World War launched on the preposterous idea that Destiny intended Germans to rule the world as a "master race."

No wonder Stormberger's printed testament on life in that future Germany under Hitler and his henchmen had Goebbels, the Nazi minister of propaganda deem it necessary to earmark his writings for the book-burning pyres of the Hitler Youth:

The free life and thought will be imprisoned and banished. Severe masters will rule and will try to get everything under their discipline. It will be a terrible time. Whoever flees should not look back.

Mirror gazing from farther back than Stormberger by some 260 years are the Second World War prophecies of Nostradamus, the first and last of these examples uses the quatrain verse indexing to hide the dates of its beginning and its end from the time frame of France's direct involvement in hostilities:

2 Q40 ([19]40?)

Shortly afterwards, not a very long interval
A great roaring storm will be raised by land and sea,
The naval battles will be greater than ever:
Fires, creatures that shoot, making more tumult.

Either he's describing the short interval of 20 years bringing a Second World War, or the (Century) "2" and Q (Quatrain) "40" in 2 Q40 stands for *February* 1940, when the Soviets turned the tide in their pyrrhic victory over Finland during the Winter War and the Finns sued for peace. The Treaty of Moscow was thus signed a few weeks into March. The prophet perhaps visualizes a future absorbed by the eyes of fellow Frenchmen yet unborn for centuries. The Winter War winds down and in February, by a "short interval" of several weeks, the French alongside British troops land in Norway to counter a Nazi invasion. The German and British fleets clash in Norwegian fiords and coastal waters in the first of many titanic battles of the Second World War. In the prophet's inner eye and ear is an eidetic vision. We can see and hear at once the "monsters" of modern war, the grinding treads of tanks, the roaring of their laboring engines. The rifle and artillery muzzle flames and tracers of battle, the thunder and thud of great guns of modern war. The war may have started in 1939, but Nostradamus' France would be invaded in [19]40 and it would fall!

EPISTLE

Great discord in the Adriatic [Italy, Yugoslavia and Greece], *warfare will arise…unions will be spit apart…including England and France in* [the year] *'45 and other* [broken unions] *in '41, '42 and '37.*

Italy, Yugoslavia and Greece all became bloody theaters of war.

Many unions and treaties were *split apart*. Hitler broke the Treaty of Versailles in 1936 with his re-occupation of the Rhineland, and his occupation of Austria in 1938—a near miss for 1937. Full-scale war broke out between China and Japan when the Marco Polo Bridge incident in July [19]*37* severed a number of agreements and truces signed with the Japanese by Chinese Nationalists under Chang Kai-shek. Hitler's invasion of Russia in [19]*41* ripped apart the notorious German-Soviet Non-Aggression Pact signed in Moscow by German Foreign Minister Ribbentrop and Soviet Foreign Minister Molotov. A cynical "union" between sworn enemies had temporarily kept Hitler's eastern flank secure and he could start the Second World War because of it. America broke long-standing trade agreements with Japan in [19]*41* when US President Roosevelt established an embargo of all US petrol and steel exports to Japan in protest of the Japanese occupying French Indochina. Japan severed any remaining agreements with a surprise attack on the US Pacific Fleet stationed in Pearl Harbor on 7 December [19]*41*.

Finally, Hitler's Axis Alliance, a union of Japan, Italy, and Germany was *split apart* by defeat in [19]*45*, punctuated by Soviet armies blasting their way into Berlin's bombed out streets to confront die-hard Nazi divisions in one of the war's bloodiest battles.

Next off, Nostradamus names Hitler.

EPISTLE

In that time and in those countries an infernal power will rise against the Church of Jesus Christ, this shall be the second Antichrist.

9 Q90

The Captain of Greater Germany will come to deliver false help,
A King of Kings, support from Pannonia [Hungary],
So that his war will cause a great shedding of blood.

The official name for Hitler's Third Reich was *Grossdeutsches Reich* (The *Greater German* Realm). Nostradamus names Hitler "Hister": his code for the second of three foreseen Antichrists. The first was Napoleon, code named *PAU, NAY, LORON,* or, *Napaulon Roy* (Napoleon King). These, and a Third and Final Antichrist (our contemporary) is the subject of my book *Nostradamus and the Antichrist, Code Named: MABUS.*

Hitler as Antichrist Two is a false messiah (*King of Kings*) seeking Hungary as an Axis ally fighting on the Eastern Front against the Soviet Union where five million Axis and 27 million Soviets soldiers and civilians died (*a great shedding of blood*). Roughly half of all fatalities suffered in the Second World War fell on the Eastern Front.

Hitler almost won his war of aggression applying a new form of mobile warfare using armies of panzer tanks called *Blitzkrieg* (Lightning War):

4 Q99

He will launch thunderbolts—so many and in such an array
Near, and far, then deep into the West.

His panzers and Stuka dive-bombers first invaded nearby Poland in September 1939, taking it down in three weeks. Then took a deep plunge of lightning war into Holland and Belgium (May 1940). Also that May, panzers rolled rapidly out of the Ardennes Forest in a surprise attack, plunging westward, deep into France.

5 Q81

The wall of the East will fall, thunder and lightning.
In seven days the enemy directly at the gates.

The *wall* is an allusion to the great string of fortresses known as the Maginot Line that Nostradamus in 4 Q80 writes is "divided by water into fifteen parts." The Maginot Line was the ONLY static defense line in history divided by 15 rivers. German troops would later break through the fortification in two places, but first they had pushed the backs of the British Expeditionary Force against the sea at Dunkirk, forcing upon them an evacuation that left most of its heavy guns, trucks and equipment abandoned on the beaches. The Germans then turned their attention back to French armies blocking their way to Paris. The offensive (Operation Red) concentrated Blitzkrieg (*lightning*-war) panzer strikes deep into France. Once unleashed on 5 June, it took Hitler's forces only "seven days" to reach the gates of Paris!

Destiny's tide would turn:

C2 Q24

Beasts wild with hunger will cross the rivers,
The greater part of the battlefield will be against Hister [Hitler].
He will cause the great one to be drawn into an iron cage,
When the child of Germany observes no law.

Nostradamus, a pre-Industrial Age prophet, returns to his descriptions of tanks, landing craft and pontoon bridge-building equipment as "beasts." Infernal mechanical beasts consumed Nazi armies in fire and smoke of soaring dragon-like planes, rumbling steel, bear-like monster tanks in a deafening, hungry gnashing of gears and treads devoured men in strobe-lit, fiery report and whining cry of tens of thousands of artillery pieces and their ordnance.

The Axis and Soviet armies fought the greatest of these battles at river crossings when the Red Army plunged over the Volga River (Stalingrad, 1942), the Neva (Siege of Leningrad, 1943), and along the length of the Dnieper (Kiev, 1943). Battles raged on both banks of the Danube at Budapest (1944) and Vienna (1945). The Danube's ancient name is *Hister*. "Hitler" grew up in Linz, Austria, on its shore, making this reference Nostradamus' double entendre covering the river battles and implicating the man who was responsible for them.

Rivers crossed by the Allies in battles on the Western Front include the liberation of Paris (the Seine) and the two great battles crossing the Rhine: Arnhem (1944) and the Battle of the Rhine (1945). The final titanic battle of the European theater had Soviet metal beasts of tank, plane and artillery carriages pass over the Oder and Neisse Rivers taking their no-quarter fight into the streets of Berlin (April-May 1945) to the roar of 20,000 Soviet artillery guns and Katyusha rocket launchers.

Photos of Hitler's Fuehrer Bunker under construction in Berlin display it just before the cement had been poured, as a vast "iron cage" assembled out of rebar. This would be the "cage" in which a trammeled Hitler ended his days.

Bartholomaeus envisaged Germans living in a psychic darkness, letting Hitler break constitutional laws. Nostradamus additionally foresaw Nazi lawlessness. The Hitler Youth organization was intended to reprogram the children of Germany into what Hitler fondly defined as modern, blond warrior barbarians, hard and merciless, brainwashed to disrespect as weakness all forms of humanitarian laws and ethics of peace-loving, civilized human beings.

Then came the downfall:

5 Q45

The great Empire will soon be desolated,
And transferred near the forest of the Ardennes:
The two bastards will be beheaded by the oldest,
Aenodarb, will rule, the hawk nosed one.

Two empires fell because of surprise Panzer Army attacks through the forest of the Ardennes. The French Colonial Empire in 1940 was transferred to the Third Reich under a Vichy puppet government administration. A little over four years later, Hitler in a desperate gamble to stop Allied forces from advancing into Germany, squandered his final strategic reserves trying a second surprise attack through the Ardennes during the Battle of the Bulge. His defeat soon after led to Germany's total surrender to the Allies in the fifth month, May, of 1945—[5] [19]45!

The two bastards executed are Mussolini by partisans and Hitler by his own hand. Aenodarb is an anagram for "red beard," it's an allusion to Hitler's favorite medieval king, Frederick Barbarossa. Nostradamus often plays with the term Barbarossa when describing Germany's war with the Soviet Union. It had begun with a surprise attack on 22 June 1941 codenamed Operation Barbarossa (Red Beard).

The *hawk nosed one*, is French General Charles De Gaulle, leader of the successful Free French Resistance. He's named outright in the following vision chronicling De Gaulle's three episodes as leader of the French people: 1) head of the Free French in 1940-1945; 2) head of the provisional French government in 1946; and, 3) President of France from 1959 until 1969:

For three times one surnamed de Gaulle will lead France. (9 Q33)

Returning to Stormberger, he is more specific in pinpointing the time between the First and Second World War.

Two or three decades after the first great war will come a second, still greater war. Almost all nations of the world will be involved. Millions of men will die, without being soldiers.

War beginning in 1939 "and/or" 1949?

I believe Stormberger was mistaking two wars as one. He accurately dated the Second World War, which did begin with Hitler's invasion of Poland on 1 September 1939, *two decades* after the First World War. The hostilities of the Cold War began around 1949 *three* decades later. Once again we have the German Stormberger viewing the future through some mysterious connection to the destiny of his own people, just like Nostradamus could see the future through the eyes of future Frenchmen. The Cold War truly began in Germany, with the Soviet blockade of the US, British and French sectors of West Berlin from all access to rail and road transport, starting on 24 June 1948. The Western allies airlifted food and materials to the ruined capital until the blockade was lifted on 12 May *1949.*

Stormberger in the riddle (*Millions of men will die, without being soldiers*), confronted a fantastic possibility, modern man only knows too well. The targets of war are not only armies but also an entire nation's civilian population. He is stating a future fact: more unarmed civilian males are killed, alongside the women victims in the *second war*. This brings to mind again the catastrophic loss of life in Russia—27-million killed, 18 million of these were civilians.

Pity the man Stormberger "outstanding" in his field (with his cows, that is), who presaged oceans of fire consume entire cities from incendiaries falling out of the bomb bay doors of the Second World War's 1000-plane Allied air fleets:

Fire will fall from the sky and many great cities will be destroyed! Whoever flees, should not look back.

The fleeing refugees could be the millions of Germans escaping from Eastern Prussia before the steamrolling advance of Soviet forces in the final death throes of the Third Reich.

He paints a picture of post-war Germany and Europe in ruins, reeking with the pestilential smell of death, with millions more displaced and the political borders of lands like Germany utterly changed:

After the great clearance, during which pestilence will tarry in the air and in the cellars and on the roofs, millions of men will have no free ground any more, no country and no home, because many cities will be no more and the frontiers of many states will be fixed anew.

In the summer of 1986, I wrote the following passage for my first published book and international bestseller *Nostradamus and the Millennium* (Doubleday-Dolphin, 1987). The world at the time was still held fast in the grip of the Cold-War mindset and nuclear standoff. The US-Soviet arms race had stockpiled a mountainous doomsday arsenal putting together a sum total of 77,000 nuclear weapons. Only a few years earlier, President Reagan had unleashed his "Evil Empire" rant and nearly came to doomsday blows with Andropov. I almost didn't put this passage in. I thought my interpretation of trends was excessively optimistic. Intuition compelled me to go ahead and I published what I felt might be an unexpectedly sudden and peaceful conclusion to the Cold War, soon.

> *There are already indications that both the US and USSR see a future when alliance between their countries would be beneficial in the light of Middle Eastern disturbances. According to Nostradamus this may happen close to the end of this decade and the way matters are progressing, the new and seemingly intelligent leader of the Soviets, Mikhail Gorbachev, may lead the way to this alliance—something certainly that could not have been predicted by this generation of communist haters in the United States, let alone by a man over four centuries before.*

Nostradamus and the Millennium, pg. 146

The key to unlocking the mysteries of Nostradamus is a deep study of the literary devices popularly used in his day. One needs to read the books Nostradamus read and thereby understand how the train of his intellectual thought processes developed. For instance, in the next quatrain written in 1555, he thinly hides the contents of one of those books written and published in Latin by an author hailing from across the English Channel, the philosopher Sir Thomas More. The following two verses may anticipate the collapse of Soviet communism putting an end to the Cold War.

3 Q95

The law of More will be seen to decline,
Followed by one more pleasing:
The Boristhenes first will give way,
Through gifts and tongues more attractive.

In the original Old French, *Morique* can stand for the Latin *More*: "custom, a practice." Likewise, *More* could be purposefully missing an "o" switched out for an "e" if Nostradamus is playing with anagrams to hide *Moor*, by extension, *Moorish* or *Muslim* law is implied. You could then apply this verse to a future decline of extreme fundamentalist interpretations of Islamic Sharia Law in the *Qur'an* undermining support for al-Qaeda and other radical jihad movements. I don't subscribe to that. Far "More" is going on here than initially meets my third eye. The weird geographical location (Boristhenes) is the key that unlocks this verse taking us to a place where few Muslims have tread.

Sometimes an interpreter of Nostradamus can miss the obvious clue that's not an anagram but a name in the clear. The *law of More* is a concept proposed by Sir Thomas More, author of *Utopia*, published in Latin in 1516 when Nostradamus was approaching his mid-teens and preparing to attend secondary education at Avignon, Provence, the following year. Indeed he might have read a copy of More's *Utopia* chained to the wall of the Avignon library, a common custom of watchful proctors of the school to guard against theft.

Utopia, is one of the first socialist manifestos ever written. Communist Russia was officially called the Union of Soviet *Socialist* Republics. *Boristhenes* is the sixteenth-century name for the Dnieper River and by extension the Ukraine region. Interpreters in the twentieth-century had not been able to decipher the importance of the Ukraine in the downfall of communism. When I was writing my first book in the spring of 1986, I became the first interpreter to offer an idea that 3 Q95 (and 4 Q32 to be examined next) foresaw the Chernobyl nuclear disaster as the impetus for ending Soviet socialism:

> *These quatrains "in progress" see first the czarist old order then communism itself replaced by a new and apparently more agreeable way of life by the end of this century… Boristhenes is the sixteenth-century name for the Dnieper River: Ukraine region. Interpreters of this century could not decipher the importance of the Ukraine in the downfall of communism. That was before Chernobyl nuclear disaster of 1986 changed the lives of one hundred thousand Ukrainians, who will live with the specter of radiation sickness for the rest of their lives.*

> *Nostradamus and the Millennium*, pg. 78

This manmade disaster of a reactor meltdown provided an opportunity and political cover that the new Premier Mikhail Gorbachev needed to provoke an honest and open reassessment of a Soviet system in decline and needing reform. Chernobyl's shock silenced the communist old guard, stopped bureaucratic resistance to change and gave Gorbachev an opportunity to clear the air and initiate *Perestroika* (Restructuring) encouraging a new "Openness" (*Glasnost*) where criticism of Soviet communism was allowed and many repressive laws were relaxed. What was intended only to reform communism led to the beginning of its end in the late 1980s when the Berlin Wall came crashing down. Eastern Europeans abandoned their socialist governments and flooded through the fallen walls, checkpoints and opened borders to visit and sample Western democracy and free market capitalism that, as the verse says, were *far more attractive.*

In *Boristhenes* could be a double pun for Ukraine and the first democratically elected president of Russia, "Boris" (Yeltsin). He became the leader of a modern Russian democracy movement that overthrew Gorbachev and communism by December 1991. In size, military and industrial power, and population the Ukraine is the most significant former Soviet Republic to break away from the USSR. *Boris* (Yeltsin) became president of the Russian Federation around the same time the *Boristhenes* (the Ukraine) became an independent sovereign state.

Nostradamus scattered his quatrains out of sequence. Yet for the initiated, there are word bridges and thematic patterns of phrase connecting the verse "puzzle" pieces to form a larger prophecy. The following quatrain is the only other taking up the socialist theme of the last:

4 Q32
In the places and times when flesh will give way to fish,
The communal law will be made in opposition:
The old order will hold strong, then are removed from the scene,
Then everything held in common between friends
[communism] *put far behind.*

39

The riddle of the first line can be solved by the return of Russian Orthodox religious traditions symbolized by the reconstruction of Moscow's greatest church, the Cathedral of Christ the Savior that Stalin had dynamited in one of his purges called the Anti-Religious Campaign in 1933. Atheism was the communist state religion—man had no soul, only "flesh." Communism in 1933 was on the rise and strong. Decades later, after Chernobyl, after Glasnost exposed for all to see how systemically decrepit Soviet communism was by the late 1980s, there was little bite-with-a-bullet-in-the-back-of-one's-head left in the geriatric Politburo. The Russian Orthodox Church was undergoing a resurrection in Russia. The church metropolitans asked and easily got permission to rebuild the cathedral, starting in 1990. The massive structure took a decade to complete. By that time the Soviet Union, communism and atheism had been eclipsed by a Christian revival.

The Soviet red banner with the golden-traced red star, hammer and sickle was lowered for the last time on the flagpole of the Kremlin on the night of Christ's birthday, 25 December 1991. Up went the white-blue-red tricolor of the new nation, The Russian Federation. The "flesh" of materialism had been supplanted in Russia, once again by those who bore the Christian symbol of the "fish."

Nostradamus, in a few words, reviews 74 years of Soviet communal law in opposition to Czar and religion. It took three revolutions in 1905, March 1917, and at last the successful Bolshevik take over in November 1917, to overturn the strength of the *old order*, the many centuries Russia existed under the autocratic power of the Czars. The communists *removed from the scene* and executed Czar Nicholas II and all his family in Siberia. Then, 74 years later, symbolically after sunset on Christmas Day, communism was *put far behind*.

Next, Nostradamus dates the Cold War's end.

2 Q89

One day the two great leaders will become friends,
Their great power will be seen to increase:
The new land [America] will be at the height of its power,
To the bloody one, the number is reported.

This prophecy prompted my 1986 leap of intuition divining an end to the Cold War at the decade's close. It seemed to me then, that Russia and the US just might end their Cold War and become friends. There is one linguistically ominous hint, however, of all goodwill efforts potentially failing. The word Nostradamus uses for *friends* in his original text is a made up word, a Greco-French hybrid, *demis*. It could be code for the French *d'amis*—friends. On the other hand, *demis* as he spells it, uncorrected, is the Greek word describing friends who will be "halved, divided, split."

The phrase "new land" appears several times in Nostradamus representing the "New World," which had only been discovered (or rediscovered) by Europeans 11 years before Nostradamus was born. In prophecies with similar New World themes, Nostradamus gets more specific calling it "Americh" (10 Q66), or like here in the above verse, he weaves a wicked linguistic and geographical pun out of *Armorique*. It usually represents the westernmost French province of Brittany, jutting like a long French nose directed into the Atlantic, bird-dogging its pointy tip right in "America's" general direction.

Sometimes, the quatrain index dates a prophecy. Century "2" becomes the second month of a year, *February*. Quatrain "89" would be [19]89. Soviet forces pulled out of Afghanistan in February 1989. The 10-year Soviet occupation and guerilla war with the Mujahedeen did much to affect the downfall of Soviet power. By December 1989, the senior President Bush (George H.W. Bush) and Soviet Premier Mikhail Gorbachev declared the Cold War officially over.

America became victor and the sole world superpower enjoying a decade of global military and economic supremacy unmatched by any nation or empire in history. The Soviet Union rapidly collapsed into the Russian Federation. Although reduced in size, Russia still straddled Europe and Asia as the largest nation on Earth. Russia, no longer isolated behind its ideological Iron Curtain, could sell its rich mineral, oil and natural gas resources in the global free market. Under the rule of Russian Federation's second President, Vladimir Putin, it enjoyed a recovery and grew into a significant military and economic power: *Their great power* [America "and" Russia] *will be seen to increase.*

The final line takes us back to 1989. The *man of blood* is the last Soviet Premier, Mikhail Gorbachev. Perhaps Nostradamus identified him by his prominent blood-splattered birthmark atop his balding head and brow. The *number* reported is the agreed amount under discussion of an eventual 75-percent reduction of Soviet and American nuclear weapons arsenals pledged by Gorbachev and Bush Sr. when they signed START (the Strategic Arms Reduction Treaty) in July 1991. That was nearly five months to the day before the Soviet Union and Gorbachev's watch, as its last premier, terminated and the Russian Federation embraced the treaty.

Four years after I wrote about possible friendship and alliances of Russia and America, the Cold War did end with hope kept alive by the genteel example of Bush Sr. and Gorbachev that many lovers of peace hoped would become the basis for sustaining a tradition of mutually assured *friendship* and collaboration of future Russian and US presidents.

Gorbachev and Bush Sr. had settled on a widely publicized gentleman's agreement about what to do about NATO (The North Atlantic Treaty Organization). Its adversary, the Warsaw Pact, had evaporated. What further need was there for NATO?

What worried Gorbachev was whether NATO would exploit the Soviet Union's weakened state and advance eastward encroaching on Russia's frontiers, converting and absorbing former Soviet satellites into their alliance. Russia historically was invaded most often from the west, it had happened twice already in the twentieth century during the First and Second World Wars. Imperial Germany with the Austro-Hungarians, then Nazi Germany with Italy, Hungary, Finland and Romania at her side murdered eight million in the First and 27 million in the Second World War. Creating distance, a territorial buffer from European invasions, was the main motivation why Stalin kept Eastern Europe in the communist bloc.

President Bush promised Gorbachev that NATO would never advance one foot eastward. The Soviet Premier, ever the gullible leader—for instance he thought loosening the grip of dictatorial power a little would save communism—believed Bush was an honorable man, though the US president didn't volunteer to back his promise in writing, making it official and binding.

Four years before Bush offered his verbal pledge, I had written about Gorbachev's role, "[He] may lead the way to this alliance—something certainly that could not have been predicted by this generation of communist haters in the United States, let alone by a man over four centuries before. But..."

The alliance does not last long.

chapter two

The Hegemonic Manifesto
And the Cold War on Terrorism
That Failed

This conjunction of an immense military establishment and a large arms industry is new in the American experience. The total influence—economic, political, even spiritual—is felt in every city, every statehouse, every office of the federal government. We recognize the imperative need for this development. Yet we must not fail to comprehend its grave implications. Our toil, resources and livelihood are all involved; so is the very structure of our society. In the councils of government, we must guard against the acquisition of unwarranted influence, whether sought or unsought, by the military–industrial complex. The potential for the disastrous rise of misplaced power exists, and will persist. We must never let the weight of this combination endanger our liberties or democratic processes. We should take nothing for granted. Only an alert and knowledgeable citizenry can compel the proper meshing of the huge industrial and military machinery of defense with our peaceful methods and goals so that security and liberty may prosper together.

US President Dwight D. Eisenhower
Farewell Address to the Nation, 17 January 1961

Power needs a relationship, a reason for being defined by an adversary, a person or a thing to feel threatened by, to struggle against—an enemy one contains and ultimately defeats after a long standoff. The righteous power without something to demonize has no context. From the Berlin Airlift in 1948-1949 to the departure 41 years later in

February 1989 of Soviet troops out of Afghanistan, the Cold War gave America a context to define itself as "the Good Guys." It was the leader of a "Free World" poised to fight if need be, but rather, preferring a vigilant containment of an "evil" Soviet empire of Communist Bloc nations.

Victory was achieved without a thermonuclear war. All prophecies and their interpreters who hectored about Armageddon being a final battle of mutually assured destruction by ICBMs had it wrong. Vast wealth was invested in an arms race to end all arm's races for four decades, crowding the planet with over 80,000 nuclear weapons, 90 percent of which were buried in missile silos or piled high in the arsenals of the US and USSR on hair-trigger alert. US missiles contained the socialist enemy while subtler weapons of Western "capital" (Latin for "head" as in capitalist free market "mind games") actually defeated them. Weapons of economics and politics had dealt the Soviet Union the *coup de grace.* There was great rejoicing around the world on Christmas Day 1991, when the hammer and sickle flag was lowered from the Kremlin roof proclaiming the Great Red enemy was dead and buried.

And yet...

Though a struggle can be sustained for a long time, the glory of final victory is fleeting. Peace long dreamed of, when it arrives at last, leaves the powerful feeling strangely flat with the bellicose "blahs."

At the end of the 1930s, the United States for the first time in its existence found itself staying in the perpetual war business, starting with arming itself for two world wars: one hot (1939-1945), the other cold (1948-1989). President Franklin Roosevelt's "Lend Lease" program began it in 1939 by loaning ships and building weapons for the British in their fight against Nazi Germany. This general retooling of the US economy to manufacture war products revitalized and reemployed its work force effectively ending the Great Depression. By the time the US directly entered the war in late 1941, it was already well prepared to exponentially increase its weapons output. Less than two years later it had transformed itself into the "arsenal of democracy," a vast military industry producing thousands of ships, tens of thousands of planes, tanks and artillery without which Allied and Soviet forces could not have defeated the Axis Alliance.

Americans generally assumed a vibrant war economy would shift gears at war's end going back to supplying goods for a booming peacetime economy. Had this not been the way before? Would there not be a peace benefit, an economic boom to follow, just like those that followed the American Civil War and the First World War?

The two world wars of the twentieth century had not ended cleanly. Germany's unfinished business in the first war prepared the way for a second world war. A Non-Aggression Pact signed by Nazi Germany and the Soviet Union helped to open hostilities. Hitler, one of the two perpetrators, had been destroyed, the other, Stalin, along with America, had fulfilled Hitler's final prophecy and transformed the Soviet Union into an adversarial superpower.

Friction and mistrust on both sides soon led to a pulling down of the Soviet Iron Curtain, dividing Europe and Germany. Even before that happened, the US began a feverish atomic arms race, initially without an opponent. By 1948 the Soviets began testing and building their own stockpile of these infernal machines, playing catch-up with the Americans who had manufactured death-times-245 atomic warheads by then.

War led to peace in 1945, and fostered a new and Orwellian doublespeak reality: war as peace—a Cold War to keep "the peace" between the American eagle and the Russian bear. The two would built peace oriented and military industrial oriented economies. However, the Soviets, because of their socialist command economics, could not profit from their war industry like the free market-oriented American economy that would successfully sustain a post-World War industry, making its middle class and corporations fabulously Cold-War wealthy.

No ordinary person watching the Soviet flag lowered in December 1991 was mourning for what that victory ended—the price of living under the threat of Armageddon's mutual US-and-Soviet annihilation, stockpiled in ready-to-launch arsenals, spring-coiled NATO and Warsaw Pact armies, air forces and fleets. No one was depressed but the powerful, that is. They were now short an enemy.

For such men, the US must find a "them" to "them-or-us" the US Send up a new bogeyman to contain—a military industrial complex to sustain. The Pax Americana coveted a new strategic philosophy. What later was called Neoconservatism first emerged in a top secret paper called the *Defense Planning Guidance*, authored by Under Secretary of Defense Paul Wolfowitz in 1992. It was leaked to the *New York Times* and the *Washington Post*. The manifesto posited a redefinition of America's mission in the post-Cold War era:

> *The number one objective of US post-Cold War political and military strategy should be...to prevent the re-emergence of a new* [US] *rival... The US must show the leadership necessary to establish and protect a new order that holds the promise of convincing potential competitors that they need not aspire to a greater role or pursue a more aggressive posture to protect their legitimate interests... We must account sufficiently for the interests of the advanced industrial nations to discourage them from challenging our leadership or seeking to overturn the established political and economic order. Finally, we must maintain the mechanisms for deterring potential competitors from even aspiring to a larger regional or global role...*

A cornerstone of this new-world-ordered thinking listed scenarios requiring the US wage aggressive, preemptive war against any rogue regimes it believed challenged its hegemonic interests:

> [A threat, subjective or empirical to deny] *access to vital raw materials, primarily Persian Gulf oil; proliferation of weapons of mass destruction and ballistic missiles, threats to US citizens from terrorism or regional or local conflict, and threats to US society from narcotics trafficking...*
>
> *If necessary, the United States must be prepared to take unilateral action...* [The US] *should expect future coalitions to be ad hoc assemblies.* [The primary importance is] *the sense that the world order is ultimately backed by the US...*

[and it] *should be postured to act independently when collective action cannot be orchestrated.*

The neocon movement once in power in Washington would later put into action these ideas. They would draw a hit list for regimes sharing one trait in common: their dictators, some of whom had once been allies of America during the Cold War such as Saddam Hussein of Iraq, threatened to stop doing business in US petrol dollars.

Wolfowitz's leaked classified memo stirred up a storm of controversy compelling President Bush Sr. to instruct then-Defense Secretary Dick Cheney to rewrite it. Wolfowitz and Cheney emerged as early apostles of neocon thinking. Removed from political power temporarily during the eight-year run of the Clinton administration, they spread the new conservative-supremacist gospel to William Kristol and Robert Kagan. These two penned the following passages (written in 1996), in a manifesto entitled *Toward a Neo-Reaganite Foreign Policy* published to celebrate the launch in 1997 of the Project for the New American Century (PNAC), a Washington, D.C. think tank that became a neoconservative Camelot.

The more Washington is able to make clear that it is futile to compete with American power, either in size of forces or in technological capabilities, the less chance there is that countries like China or Iran will entertain ambitions of upsetting the present world order... The United States achieved its present position of strength not by practicing a foreign policy of live and let live, nor by passively waiting for threats to arise, but by actively promoting American principles of governance abroad—democracy, free markets, respect for liberty... Support for American principles around the world can be sustained only by the continuing exertion of American influence...And sometimes that means not just supporting US friends and gently pressuring other nations but actively pursuing policies in Iran, Cuba, or China, for instance—ultimately intended to bring about a change of regime... History also shows, however,

that the American people can be summoned to meet the chal-
lenges of global leadership if statesmen make the case loudly,
cogently, and persistently… Republicans are surely the genu-
ine heirs to the Reagan tradition… Conservatives these days
succumb easily to the charming old metaphor of the United
States as a "city on a hill." They hark back…to the admonition
of John Quincy Adams that America ought not go "abroad in
search of monsters to destroy." But why not? The alternative is
to leave monsters on the loose, ravaging and pillaging to their
hearts' content, as Americans stand by and watch… Because
America has the capacity to contain or destroy many of the
world's monsters, most of which can be found without much
searching, and because the responsibility for the peace and se-
curity of the international order rests so heavily on America's
shoulders, a policy of sitting atop a hill and leading by ex-
ample becomes in practice a policy of cowardice and dishonor.
A true "conservatism of the heart" ought to emphasize both
personal and national responsibility, relish the opportunity for
national engagement, embrace the possibility of national great-
ness, and restore a sense of the heroic.

One could read the above as an American clarion call similar to *Deutschland Erwachen!* (Germany Awaken!), the slogan of the new Germany of the 1930s.

"America Awaken!" to a new US supremacist world order. Ask not that America live by example, ask that America contain any threat by whatever unilateral means, as a law above international laws if neces-sary, to cold heartedly, preemptively, suppress or aggressively destroy any opposition to those who it had judged are "monsters" or "dragons" to slaughter for the greater good.

A heroic, neoconservative America need not explain itself to lesser mortals or defend its actions.

Amerika über alles!

Even liberals would later get on board in the "new American cen-tury" with a little more lofty and flowery variation on this renewed

American exceptionalism. It defines "us" who call ourselves "U.S." of A as a benign, though ultimately powerful, force promoting our higher idea of what freedom, democracy and free market economies are according to definitions flexible enough to change according to our "noble" needs. We instruct you to listen only to what we *say*, look away from what we *do* to the world. Trust us, we are an exceptional people who can go beyond excepted limits to unilaterally invade and occupy other countries. *Yes we can* apply vigorously a necessary shock-and-awe inspiring evil of war for the greater good of *our* New World Order that we have invited—no! we compel *you*—to live under without question.

The presidential election of 2000 rekindled hopes for an ideologically sympathetic president to replace Clinton. Governor of Texas George W. Bush, the son of the 41st President, seemed to be their malleable man. He would win the notoriously disputed vote recount in Florida against Vice President Al Gore and soon surround himself with a who's who of a neoconservative infiltrated cabinet, such as Karl Rove (President G.W. Bush's chief political advisor and head of the Office of the White House Office of Strategic Affairs); Richard Armitage (US Deputy Secretary of State); Dick Cheney (Vice President of the United States); Zalmay Khalilzad (later becoming first US ambassador to the post-Saddam Hussein Iraq during the US occupation); Lewis "Scooter" Libby (special assistant to the Vice President); Richard Perle (Chairman during the G.W. Bush Administration of the Defense Policy Board Advisory Committee); Donald Rumsfeld (Secretary of Defense); and Paul Wolfowitz (Deputy Secretary of Defense).

"We have a plan for Iraq," winked the president-to-be (the candidate the Supreme Court later chose for Americans by overturning the Florida State Supreme Court's ruling to recount the entire state vote). Bush made this statement in the first of three nationally televised presidential debates held in early October 2000.

The month before had seen published a report entitled *Rebuilding America's Defenses*, written by Kristol, Kagan and the future Deputy Secretary of Defense, Paul Wolfowitz. These think tank gurus and elder statesmen, along with Dick Cheney, had intensified their coaching of an often-clueless candidate Bush on foreign policy matters as the debates and election drew close. He had already made famous gaffs in press interviews betraying a lack of knowledge about world politics and leaders. Twice Bush said the former General Pervez Musharraf, then President of Pakistan, was simply named "General".

Perhaps Bush's smirk and winking about a plan for Iraq echoed Chapter V of the September 2000 neoconservative paper entitled: *Creating Tomorrow's Dominant Force*:

> *While the unresolved conflict in Iraq provides the immediate justification* [for US military presence], *the need for a substantial American force presence in the* [Persian] *Gulf transcends the issue of the regime of Saddam Hussein… Over the long term, Iran may well prove as large a threat to US interests in the Gulf as Iraq has. And even should US-Iranian relations improve, retaining forward-based forces in the region would still be an essential element in US security strategy given the longstanding American interests in the region.*
>
> *…Further, the process of transformation, even if it brings revolutionary change, is likely to be a long one, absent some catastrophic and catalyzing event—like a new Pearl Harbor.*

Eight months into his presidency on 11 September 2001 al-Qaeda jihadists hijacked four jets, two of which flew crews and passengers held hostage, into the World Trade Center towers in New York City. Another plunged through the western wall of the Pentagon building in Washington, DC. A fourth, chosen to cave in the US Capitol building dome, crashed in a farming field outside of Pittsburgh.

On 10 September 2012, *Vanity Fair* contributing editor Kirt Eichenwald wrote an Op-ed for the *New York Times* entitled *The Deafness Before the Storm*. He claims President G.W. Bush had received several unquestionably clear, top secret warnings from US intelligence sources above and beyond the well-known 6 August 2001 classified intelligence brief raising an alarm about Usama bin Laden's terrorist network al-Qaeda, and that they were "determined to strike the US." The Bush administration was also warned of the developing attack in the spring of 2001 in direct situation reports delivered on 1 May 2001 and later 22 June 2001 concluding al-Qaeda strikes were "imminent." Again the CIA on 29 June briefed the president on "dramatic consequences" of a near-term attack with massive casualties. On 1 July 2001 intelligence memos forewarned Bush that an attack would happen soon. On 24 July the president was told the attack was still on track for launch but postponed for a few months, meaning that the danger of domestic attack would return by September. In August, the president went on a month-long vacation at his Crawford Ranch in Texas where he received, with chief cabinet members, Condoleezza Rice (NSA), Vice President Cheney, the much-publicized 6 August CIA briefing.

Bill Clinton's last moment in power as president, his parting statement after eight years in office, was spent advising Bush to establish as his first national security priority, stifling and destroying the emerging threat of Usama bin Laden and his al-Qaeda terrorist organization. Nothing Clinton said, or what the CIA's secret briefings explained, stuck with President Bush. No suggestion to prepare for the attack on the homeland, such as raising military defense readiness, was forthcoming from those surrounding Bush, such as neoconservative Vice President Cheney and Under Secretary of Defense Paul Wolfowitz or the platoon of other neocons in his cabinet. Apologists blame the lack of action on inattentiveness, mediocrity even—similar to the lack of vigilance of a nation at peace before the Japanese made their surprise carrier-born attack on the US Pacific Fleet anchored in the shallows of Peal Harbor.

Either by accident or by a conspiracy of omission, the neoconservatives in the White House got their "new Pearl Harbor" on 11 September 2001. As hoped by the purveyors of *Creating Tomorrow's Dominant Force* the unskeptical, "follow-the-leader" bipartisan support out of US Congress and a traumatized nation was achieved to speed up the accomplishment of neoconservative goals. The first casualty of war was reasonable criticism directed at the Bush administration. The question gone unasked was, how could the Bush administration allow a domestic terrorist attack never before experienced on this scale happen on their watch? Neither did anyone ask why President Bush, a week out from the 9-11 attacks, had already named this new world conflict a "war on terror," nor question why he could predict how long it would last: "30 years or more." Why was this war so vaguely defined, and why was it already being sold by the White House as some kind of low-grade and long-lasting Cold War conflict?

US General Wesley Clark (Ret.), former NATO Supreme Allied Commander in Europe (1997-2000), had gone to visit Secretary of Defense Donald Rumsfeld and Under Secretary of Defense Paul Wolfowitz at the Pentagon ten days after a hijacked civilian airliner drilled into its western façade. He related his experience to Amy Golden of *Democracy Now* on 2 March 2007 in a packed auditorium. The YouTube video has since gone viral.

> *I went down stairs just to say hello to some of the people on the Joint* [Chiefs of] *Staff who used to work for me and one of the Generals called me in and said "Sir, you have ah... Come in. You've got to come in and talk to me for a second."*
>
> *I said, "Well, you're too busy."*
>
> *And he said, "No, No..." And he said* [with emphasis]*, We've made the decision, we're going to war with Iraq."*
>
> *This was on or about the twentieth of September* [2001]*.*
>
> *I said, "We're going to war with Iraq? Why?!"*
>
> *He said, "I don't know."*
>
> *He said, "I guess they don't know what else to do."*
>
> *So, I said, "Well, did they find some information connecting Saddam to al-Qaeda?"*
>
> *He said, "No, no. There is nothing new that way, they just made the decision to go to war with Iraq."*
>
> *He said, "I guess it's, like, we don't know what to do about terrorists, but...we've got a good military and we can take down governments."*
>
> *So I came back to see him a few weeks later and by that time we were bombing in Afghanistan.*
>
> *I said, "Are we still going to war with Iraq?"*
>
> *And he said, "Oh, it's worse than that."*

He reached over on his desk and picked up a piece of paper.

He said, "I just got this down from upstairs from the Secretary of Defense's office today."

And he said, "This is a memo that describes how we are going to take out seven countries in five years. Starting with Iraq and then Syria, Lebanon, Libya, Somalia, Sudan and then finishing off Iran."

[Amy Goodman] *"Go through the countries again?"*

[Wesley Clark] *"Well, starting off with Iraq, then Syria and Lebanon, then Libya, then Somalia and Sudan and back to Iran."*

On 29 January 2002, Bush himself famously beat the war drum loudly in his nationally televised State of the Union speech before both houses of Congress. He said Iraq, along with Iran and North Korea, was building atomic weapons and constituted an "Axis of Evil arming to threaten the peace of the world."

The lesser demon regimes listed by the Bush administration lined up with many of the states targeted for overthrow appearing on the same memo neocon Secretary of Defense Donald Rumsfeld issued that General Wesley Clark had had pushed under his nose at the Pentagon a few weeks after the 9-11 attacks. It identified Syria and Libya along with Cuba as terrorist sanctioning and harboring states.

It so happens that Nostradamus' prophecies indexed as 3 Q61, 5 Q25, 10 Q72 and his prose prophecy letter, *The Epistle*, defined future (Middle) *Easterners* as a secret triumvirate of pirate (terrorist) rogue nations. The first is *Mesopotamia* (modern Iraq), the second, *Persia* (modern Iran), and the third is called *the Great Mongol*. It could be China or the rogue Stalinist throwback state North Korea, a third member of G.W. Bush's "Axis of Evil" after Iran and Iraq. North Korea's citizens are directly related to Mongolians. 10 Q72 predicts the rise of a "great Mongol" applying a sixteenth-century European habit of mixing up Mongolians with Chinese because thirteenth-century warlord Genghis Khan and his Mongolian descendants ruled from China at the heart of their greater Mongolian empire. The conceptual mindset of the "yellow peril" was born in European thinking because the Sino-Mongolian Empire came closer to conquering European civilization than any other Asian invader.

10 Q72

In the year 1999 and seven months,
The great King of Terror will come from the sky.
He will bring back the Khan of the Mongols.
Before and after Mars rules happily.

Nostradamus utilizes this metaphor to describe the rise of a future Sino-Mongolian king and empire comprised of China and many equally dangerous Muslim kingdoms as its vassals "in the year 1999 and seven months." Taking the date at face value, the new China began its meteoric rise around the turn of the century to rival the economic power of America. Look deeper at the dating: "in the year 1999 and *seven months*" (*sept mois* in Old French). September was once the calendar's seventh month until it was pushed forward, becoming the ninth because of the creation of months *July* and *August,* named after Roman Emperors *Julius* Caesar and Caesar *Augustus.* Thus its new arrangement as "1999 and *September* month" leads a translator to consider that maybe the year is in code as well. 1999 might hide the intended year. Switch the digit *one* into a *nine,* make the *three nine* digits *three ones* and 1999 becomes 9111 for 9-11-11, the 11 *September* attack date for the "Pearl Harbor" event of a new cold war on general terrorism.

From the war business angle, it goes without saying: a new 30-year threat of Islamo-Fascist terror groups, exaggerated or real, would keep the wheels of a huge military industrial complex turning out weapons in a containment-of-war business nearly as long as assembly lines rolled out products to contain communism for 42 years. The "war on terror" was a broad target package set to kill nebulous enemies with an obscurely defined strategic goal. Exactly "what" terror are we talking about and "who" is our enemy? Is it "anybody" we brand a "terrorist"? Can the definition and the mission creep through the decades from killing Muslims to assassinating domestic "terrorists"—whoever the government at the time says they are? Today American citizens who are Islamists living abroad are drone drilled with a missile. Home grown protesters of tomorrow, maybe?

It just takes a keypad punch from an armchair pilot guiding a winged robot from an office cubbyhole sequestered away in a top secret "war on terror" command center, free of and far beyond public scrutiny, to reconfigure his or her aim of a drone missile at American citizens at home.

Nostradamus in the Epistle enlarges his prescient tale of "two great leaders" of 2 Q89 (in the year 1989):

EPISTLE

And when shall the lords be two in number, victorious in the north against the [Middle] Eastern ones, there shall be a great noise and warlike tumult that all the East shall quake for fear of those two brothers of the North who are not yet brothers.

The two lords are America and Russia, doubtlessly victorious in wars waged against international terror and terrorist-sheltering nations during the 1990s. The Russian Federation had brought the spread of Islamist extremism to a standstill "against the Eastern ones," in this case the Chechen rebels in the Caucasus region. The US formed a vast international land-air-and-sea coalition of 600,000 soldiers to contain Saddam Hussein's invasion and occupation of Kuwait (1990). Then followed in early 1991 a *great noise and warlike tumult* for two months of US-coalition airstrikes devastating the military and civilian infrastructure of Iraq. The coalition had free rein, blasting Iraq back into the Stone Age as if they were like Marians gamboling across the scorched countryside in their tripod machines as imagined by H.G. Wells' with death rays held in many tentacles, invading the Earth, burning out Lilliputian popgun armies in his book *The War of the Worlds*. The ground campaign of Operation Desert Storm came next, a one-sided rout of Iraqi forces in Kuwait and southern Iraq—its massacre of retreating Iraqi forces caught in a huge traffic jam on the route out of Kuwait so biblically complete and terrible, George Bush's father ordered all ground operations stand down only 100 hours into the wholesale slaughtering.

EPISTLE

They [the Americans] *will be victorious against the Easterners.*

The quaking in fear of shock-and-*awe*-full aerial attacks on Iraq and other Easterners targeted would become an incessant, 12-year prelude to the Cold War on Terror following up the Persian Gulf War (1991) with further punitive airstrikes on Saddam Hussein's regime trapped under a "No-Fly Zone" from December 1992 to March 2003. The US military Industrial Complex was humming to fill orders for new bombs and new weapons systems from the Pentagon and lock and load allies surrounding Iraq, like Saudi Arabia, the Gulf States and Israel, with a steady stream of multi-billion-dollar weapons deals.

Contain the Iraqi regime, then kill it in a flash and flame of "shock and awe"-tsim called Operation Iraqi Freedom, the US unilateral invasion and occupation of Iraq. Victory was swift. The American juggernaut "blitzkrieged" Saddam Hussein's regime in Baghdad like Hitler's finest panzer warriors racing down the road on their way to Paris in 1940. The regime was destroyed in less than eight weeks. President Bush on May Day 2003 had flown down from the clouds, stepped out of his Air Force flight suit, donned a civvy suit and straightened his tie to declare on an aircraft carrier's flight deck, parked in safe waters off San Diego, "My fellow Americans, major combat operations in Iraq have ended. In the battle of Iraq, the United States and our allies have prevailed." (Read, "Iraq" crossed off the neocon list, six more to go.) Plans were already in full swing to find a reason to bomb Iran.

Weapons of mass destruction, the pretext for the invasion, were nowhere to be found. The Iraqi occupation became an ill-planned, socially-disordered quagmire and then a full-blown sectarian civil war between Sunni minority and Shia majority populations with the US forces in the crossfire. Bush and his neocon cabinet made one repetitive strategic mistake after another not able to process reality through their ideological filters. For instance, decades of effort to keep Islamic extremists on the fringes of the Middle East were dashed when Bush taunted al-Qaeda with an invitation to start a "new front" in Iraq. They did, flooding in from Central Asia, bringing their Jihad into the heartland of the Muslim Middle *Easterners'* world where they spread terror from Iraq in the 2000s and then into Syria in the 2010s.

No matter, quagmires can sometimes be equal to containment as a good military business model sustaining orders of weapons. Good for the coffin-building business too, and for funeral homes. Think of the profits gained from losses in the Pentagon's quagmire business model.

Iraq? Vietnam it!

The twelve thousand helicopters that were shot down or crashed in the Vietnam War is a human tragedy, but look on the bright side, the flaming wrecks that cremated many of their crews were product replacement orders in the making. It doesn't matter who's containing whom in a stalemate, as long as it keeps feeding the orders for manufacturing weapons and making war profiteers fantastically rich on the taxpayers' coin. For instance, if Humvees couldn't survive the blast of roadside bombs in Afganistan and Iraq, no problem. Have taxpayers shed billions to build a new fleet of MRAP (Mine-Resistant Ambush Protected) vehicles, sold at exorbitant prices to MRAP-around army soldiers and Marines with more blast-resistant armored personnel carriers.

Eastern kings, branded an Axis of Evil, did quake with the shock-and-awe*daciousness* of Bush's unilateral action to take down Saddam Hussein. Gaddafi voluntarily took Libya out of the nuclear weapons business in late 2003. Evidence from US intelligence sources later revealed Iran had abandoned its nuclear weapons program in 2004.

Lebanon was next on the neocon list (read, the destruction of Hezbullah, a Shi'a Islamist militant group and political party based in Southern Lebanon). In 2006, Hezbullah fired rockets into Northern Israel paving the way for an opportunity. The Israelis pummeled southern Lebanese cities all the way north to Beirut, rendering its southern high-rise suburbs into southern Swiss cheese with US manufactured military-industrial-strong, long-range artillery rounds and rockets. They blasted Hezbullah's network of underground fortifications and rocket batteries with over 800 thermoberic bunker-busted bombs bought from and exported to Israel from US munitions corporations.

True, Israel couldn't defeat Hezbullah. They lived to fight another day. Still, the war biz was abuzz with Washington signing a hefty arms deal with Tel Aviv, replacing all the highly expensive ordnance fired on Lebanon to the tune of high profiteering in the US. This shipment of more sophisticated US bombs aided Israel in flash-burning Syria's infant nuclear program with an airstrike on 6 September 2007 on an atomic research reactor under construction in the Deir ez-Zore region.

Iran was the next target that needed a nudge, an incident. US carrier strike groups began crowding the Persian Gulf from 2006 through 2008, taunting the Iranians with demonstrations of might, parading back and forth through the narrow Strait of Hormuz. Ayatullah baiting failed. Tehran never bit on the hook. The Pentagon attack package of 8,000 military and civilian targets would have to wait for a new president and new entrapment schemes. Still, the bellicose business of containment in the Persian Gulf was hotter than the interior of warehouses that were soon plugged with multiplying stockpiles of US weapons and fuel in US installations popping up all along the Arab Gulf States across the water opposite Iran.

Easterners quaked in late 2001: the Taliban, cast out of Afghanistan, and al-Qaeda core fighters scattered off the slopes of Tora Bora by B-52 carpet bombing both hurried into exile across the mountainous border with Pakistan. That move not only favored keeping the War on Terror going for another decade but it also inspired a new military sportsman's industry. Fire your bolts from the sky in a perpetually open drone-hunting season on al-Qaeda and Taliban "game" creeping from rock to mud hut. The turbaned-turkey shoot is well into its second decade of profit hunting and gathering up Washington DC military contracts.

The US Supreme Court in 2010 had defined corporations as people and those "people" in Washington actively lobby Congress and look for contractors to assemble a non-human, inhuman warrior of the future. They design and construct robot planes free of the human limitations set by US constitutional and international laws. Corporations may conveniently become people so that their android warriors need not worry about laws, like the US War Powers Act that give Congress the power to protecting living soldiers from being rashly sent to die in foreign military adventures. This new loophole spreads the war market gold rush, transforming the counties of states surrounding the District of Columbia into a golden ring of power and riches—a haven for the most billionaires per capita in America. Most of these government contractors are in the weapons business, and death, not peace, is their profession, supplying the Cold War on Terror demand.

Nostradamus, in his original Old French, defines the Brothers *of the North* as *d'Aquilon* using a classical metaphor. In the times of Ancient Rome, the Constellation of Aquila rising out of the north-by-northwestern horizon in late autumn sent a cold northern wind whistling around the pillars and into the pagan temples of Rome, rustling the pallas and togas of shivering citizens worshipping and making sacrifices. It kicked the last rusty leaves of fall down the cobblestones of the Roman Forum, signifying winter was on the way. Thus the Brothers are Northerners because Aquila "the Eagle" shines brightest over them. They are the Epistle's *great lords two in number* that straddle the Arctic Ocean: Russia, in a sweeping arc across nine time zones along its northern coast and America along its Alaskan coastline. They're the brothers the Epistle qualifies as *not yet brothers*; in other words, they are *two great leaders*, Bush Sr. and Gorbachev, of 2 Q89, trying to become friends (or, *demis*, Nostradamus' double pun for friend/split and halved). They agreed to end their Cold (winter-like frosty) War in 1989, dated in verse 89 (1989) of Century 2.

Nostradamus often used animal totems to describe future nations. The French, after their Revolution, are called "the cock" for the rooster often depicted on the regimental tricolored battle flags in early battles that pitted the French National Guard against an array of European coalition armies in the French Revolutionary Wars (1792-1802). Italy, in all times since 1555, is called "the wolf" after the classical Latin myth about the creation of Ancient Rome. Nostradamus had seen the same statues in the late 1540s that tourists marvel at today when he passed through Renaissance Italy gathering his occult tools and knowledge to prophesy. These statues depict the babies Romulus and Remus being suckled by a she-wolf. Romulus was the founder of Rome.

America has a bald eagle as its national totem, yet the Soviet Union held aloft a red star with a hammer and sickle on a red banner as its totem. Only after the collapse of the Soviet Union, partially reconstructed again as the Russian Federation, did the red star banner disappear, replaced by a new and refreshed ensign of the Czarist emblem of St. George slaying a dragon, over which is perched a great golden and double-headed Russian eagle. Russia and America did not together become *d'Aquilon*/of-the-Eagle *Northern* Kings until Russia hoisted its new double-eagle flag for the first time in 1992. That makes Nostradamus' future time "our" time starting in 1992.

Up to the mid-2010s the focus of neocons and exceptionalists on Russia growing in power and stature had been distracted by their obsession with, and setbacks mounting because of, their new cold "War on Terror." Military industrial markets began their long road to ruin when Bush invaded Iraq in 2003. Nostradamus foresaw this:

3 Q61
The great host and sect of cross bearers [or: the Crusaders],
Will be massed in Mesopotamia [Iraq]:
Of the nearby river [the Euphrates] *the fast company,*
That such a law will hold for the enemy.

Mesopotamia is the ancient Greek name for modern Iraq defined as *Meso* (between) *potamia* (rivers: the Tigris and Euphrates). During the great crusades of medieval times, no army of knights displaying the Christian cross emblazoned on surcoats draped over chain-mailed chests, set foot on Mesopotamian deserts or advanced over river wadis. Hundreds of thousands of "Crusaders," however, did pour over its frontiers, fighting and dying there from 2003 through 2011. No one disputes that a majority of men and women in this mostly US-led coalition identified themselves as a staunch Christian band of warrior brothers and sisters. The label "Crusaders" sticks because President

Bush let fly the indelicate label when announcing his 30-year "war on terror."

Bush defined the War on Terror as a "Great Crusade." His speech-writers stole the phrase from General Eisenhower's D-Day announcement speech, clueless of the offense it would stir among allies and enemies alike, across the Muslim world. The Crusaders' war crimes and messianic misdemeanors committed on the Arabs a thousand years ago are wounds still festering fresh and unforgotten. Usama bin Laden, the leader of al-Qaeda, turned Bush's label into a spiteful invective for the Western infidel enemy.

Of the nearby river (the Euphrates) *the fast company* (the US armored *blitzkrieg*-lightning fast invasion) ran its armor columns along its west bank before two pincers crossed several points southwest of Baghdad, seizing the capital in the deepest and fastest panzer penetration in military history. Of course, unlike Hitler's panzer divisions, these Americans with their similarly designed helmets weren't up against millions of Soviet soldiers with 10,000 tanks. The Iraqi Army, after joining in a few skirmishes, evaporated into the cities. Many of them followed a long-rehearsed plan to don civilian garb and start a guerrilla war.

After eight years, eight months, three weeks and four days of sustained military industrial profits collected at home, the US war market in Iraq shut down. US troops had passed back over the same Kuwaiti borders in December 2011 from whence they came in March 2003. As they had invaded, so they stole away, under the cover of darkness. In the latter case, better to shield themselves from the rocks, stones, thrown shoes and easier-to-target IED roadside explosions hastening an ignominious departure in broad daylight down the road to Kuwait.

Death also made a killing: 6,000 civilian contractors, mercenaries and US soldiers. Injury also profited: 32,000 wounded—half of them seriously crippled. Stuff the graves of American and Coalition dead with Death's bonus of 120,000 to 600,000 Iraqis killed. Leave Sickness and also Deformity a lingering stipend: generations of Iraqi children suffering radiological mutations and illness from all those highly profitable depleted uranium shells and bullets fired through Iraqi homes, planting themselves in farmland, rivers, and poisoning the water table.

Nostradamus predicted the Crusaders would lose in Mesopotamia because of *such a law* that would *hold for the enemy* of those departing Crusaders. That "law" is the Islamic Sharia, the holy law set down by the Prophet Muhammad in the *Qur'an* as a code of virtuous living for all faithful believers of Allah, only this time as it is severely interpreted by the Iraqi insurgent jihadist militias, be they warring members of the Sunni or Shia sect.

With one war market down, the next to run a war profiteering loss will be Afghanistan soon after the departure of all US combat troops and NATO allies scheduled for the end of 2014. The old bellicose business model of Vietnamization was utilized again in Iraq and Afghanistan to keep profits flowing through the rearming and training of indigenous armies, probably ending up with the same bankrupted result: a rapid collapse of Iraqi and Afghan militaries a few years after the US combat forces bug out.

The US Military Industrial Complex may have already started its ✓ "pivot," exploring new containment scenarios. War market, forward march! Next stop, the Asian Pacific region. The next military supply will go to fill the demand to contain China, even though at present the buildup is slow and war profits lean.

Certainly there was some hope to squeeze more war profits out of the Middle East during the Obama years. The containment of Iran, initially scored to date the most profitable foreign US arms deal in history: a $76-billion dollar upgrade of Saudi Arabia's defense forces. Sizable weapon-package deals hauled in the treasure as well, drained from Gulf States Bahrain, UAE and Qatar.

The Middle Eastern war market recently stirred again with some renewed life, or rather, more death. The Arab Spring demonstrations and revolutions of 2011 soon developed some promising strife and civil wars from which to choose a side and contrive an income of transnational-billions of bucks by exploiting warfare in Syria and Libya. Bush's successor Barack Obama had married his liberally exceptionalist hegemonic urges to neoconservative thinking. He struck down another rogue regime on the neoconservative list, that of Libyan strongman Muhammar Gaddafi, under the umbrella of a UN-sanctioned, new variation on the Iraqi no-fly zone strategy used this time around to bomb the combatants and collaterally damage and kill non-combatants sympathetic to Gaddafi's regime.

Next, the Obama administration tried an old Bush trick with a new angle: get American citizens to sign off on bombing yet another Middle Eastern country, this time Syria under the rule of the Bashar al-Assad dictatorship. Charge that they used weapons of mass destruction. The opportunity arose when on 21 August 2013, a Sarin gas attack on an eastern suburb of Damascus killed over 1,400 and injured 7,000 civilians sympathetic to the Free Syrian Army. Like before with Iraq, the State Department accusations flew fast, hyperbolic and unsubstantiated that "Saddam" (oh, sorry, I mean Assad) had launched his missiles of mass destruction. At least Bush's Secretary of State, Colin Powell, had to cook up some graphs, maps and flashed his vial of fake Anthrax under the noses of a public congressional hearing in October 2002. John Kerry in September 2013 just bellowed accusations without proof. In the Obama era, Congress locked doors and kept secret from the public what "proof" they were shown, necessitating a "punitive" and sustained airstrike on Assad's military and political assets.

Syria was a rehash of Libya. As before, the dog Obama picked in this fight, the Free Syrian Army, was losing the civil war just like US-backed Benghazi insurgents fighting against Gaddafi. The time had come to find any legally sanctioned or unilateral excuse to bomb the crap out of Assad's military assets like Washington did against Gaddafi's, maybe with the same result: regime change. Cross Syria off that neoconservative (and now, neo-liberal supremacist) list of seven rogues-to-render-dead regimes.

No weapons of mass destruction were found in Iraq. In Syria, however, a dangerous array of WMDs were well documented, but as Seymour Hersh disclosed (Read "The Red Line and the Rat Line," published in the *London Review of Books*, 17 April 2014), evidence mounts implying a "false flag" attack attributed to the Assad regime was in play. The missile fragments recovered at the crime (against humanity) scene could not have flown nine miles, the distance to pro-Syrian government frontlines. The size and make of the missile had a range of only five miles. That means it had been fired well within rebel held territories.

Hersh claims he uncovered a plot by al-Nusra Front, an al-Qaeda ✓ sympathetic jihadist faction, with Turkish secret service agents who acquired captured Syrian missile ordnance topped with Sarin warheads. The al-Nusra jihadists then fired on civilians sympathetic to secular Free Syrian Army factions. Hence al-Nusra killed one set of enemies, the secularist insurgents, to pull in a NATO-US airstrike, hobbling another enemy, Assad, thus ensuring what they intended would be a jihadist victory in the civil war against his regime.

If it weren't for John Kerry's off-handed "joke" at a press conference in London on 9 September 2013, no diplomatic breakthrough would have been forthcoming to tie together the left and right's shoestrings of an advancing neocon war plan. Kerry had quipped that Assad could avoid the airstrikes only if he surrendered ALL of his weapons of mass destruction.

"Of course Assad isn't about to do it and it can't be done," snarked Kerry in an afterthought.

Within 24 hours, Russian President Putin had spoken with Assad. He convinced the Syrian leader to take the joke as a serious offer, preventing a war rubbing out Russia's last remaining ally from the Soviet era in the region. Assad was glad to hand over all of his weapons under stringent United Nations observation. At the time of this writing (May 2014) nearly 90 percent of all Assad's WMD have been itemized, accounted for and handed over to the UN for shipment to a designated place of destruction on EU territory. The acts of good faith, speed and efficiency by Damascus make this event one of the UN's foremost disarmament success stories. The accomplishment is no less remarkable as it was achieved in the crossfire of a very bloody civil war that took a wrecking ball to Syria in the last three years, killing nearly 200,000 people so far and sent millions of Syrians into internal and external exile.

Kerry on the following day after his quip misstep, held a press conference to grumble that he was only joking and advised Assad and
Putin not to take his joke as a peace offer. Airstrikes were imminent!
By the end of the day it was clear Kerry was outmaneuvered. Putin
had thrown Obama a line over the hawkish secretary and the State
Department, saving the White House from a commitment to launch
airstrikes on Syria after losing all international and domestic support.

Peace was in the air and war profiteers braced to take a hair cut
financially. Alongside the first real attempt to negotiate a political settlement between Syrian factions, Kerry's "joke diplomacy" additionally
thawed a 34-year ice age in US-Iranian relations. Direct talks between
the two nations ensued and by November 2013, an interim agreement
was set for a six-month trial run, starting from 20 January to 20 July.
It would objectively test good faith in increments. Iran was ready to
prove it wasn't seeking the manufacture and proliferation of nuclear
weapons. In return, America "in good faith" lifted some UN and US
sanctions that were crippling Iran's economy.

The Cold War on Terror was faltering. It was growing quite clear
in the light of this new hope for a brotherhood of Kings of the North
being "friends" that neoconservatives had miscalculated the threat
from Russia to their hegemonic, long-term war marketing goals, even
though a neglected plan for regime change in Russia had been drafted
as early as 18 February and published on 8 March 1992 as the *Defense
Planning Guidance for the Fiscal Years 1994-1999*, written by one of neoconservatism's original ancestors, Under Secretary of Defense Paul
Wolfowitz:

> √ *Our first objective is to prevent the re-emergence of a new rival,
> either on the territory of the former Soviet Union or elsewhere,
> that poses a threat on the order of that posed formerly by the
> Soviet Union. This is a dominant consideration underlying
> the new regional defense strategy and requires that we endeavor
> to prevent any hostile power from dominating a region whose
> resources would, under consolidated control, be sufficient to
> generate global power.*

The early neocon manifestos had understandably focused little on what was left of the Soviet Colossus after 1992, that had collapsed in on itself, was divided and greatly weakened presided over by a drunken clown as its first president, Boris Yeltsin. Strategically speaking, they were long to at last come around to Russia's rise, focusing as they did obsessed with Pearl-Harbor baiting overthrows of Middle Eastern rogue regimes overtop a much coveted Garden of crudely oiled Eden.

In the meantime, Russia had changed presidents. Vladimir Putin seemed to come out of nowhere as an odd choice picked by Yeltsin as his successor: some former "flunk-functionary" perhaps of the defunct-for-a-decade KGB Soviet secret services. The drunk's choice showed far more foresight and intelligence than Western leaders and their think tanks ever respected. Putin emerged as ailing Boris Yeltsin resigned, becoming acting President of Russia in 1999. He won his first full term as president in 2004 with 71 percent of the vote and began Russia's successful economic turnaround and reconstruction serving a second term as president (2004-2008), then prime minister under President Medvedev (2008-2012), and then as president for a third term (2012-Present).

Putin turned out to be a more successful modern "Czar" hiding behind the title "president" than anyone in the West anticipated. Nostradamus' prophecy could have warned them of that in 2 Q89, which said, "both" America's power "and" Russia's "would be seen to grow." Russia just took a little more time. It remolded and modernized a far smaller though leaner and meaner military. Its economy boomed as well, utilizing its great wealth of natural resources, its oil and its natural gas exports. Russia, the greatest exporter of natural gas, keeps the European Union warm in the winter. It lights the German economy's pilot light just as German financing sustains the European Union and in return makes deep investments in building factories in Russia.

Uniquely straddled between the East and West, Putin's new Russia renewed and enlarged its highly profitable energy deals with a booming, energy-starved Chinese economy. To a liberal exceptionalist or neo-conned mindset it would look a lot like Putin was renewing the Soviet Bloc alliance with Communist Red China. Putin's touch, however, is not that of a military hegemon like America neoconservatives' project. Putin may be an oligarchic and autocratic leader overseeing a plutocracy, but he leads his people towards supplying a demand for peaceful industries producing high profits. Though Russia has expanded its armament industry, it is a modest enterprise compared to the Soviet military industrial complex and is nothing like the current US Military industrial complex devouring one fifth of the government budget each year. The US never let go of its Cold War thinking nor downsized its treasury-draining budget increases. Military expenditures, added to homeland security demands, draw one trillion dollars per annum. ALL other military budgets on this planet put together don't come close to this gluttony of spending.

Putin has often reminded the Americans, especially the warmongering neocons in office, how long ago the Cold War ended. He claims we are all living in a globally interconnected and far more peaceful world. Russia is a very different country than the Soviet Union once was. It is no longer a weak remnant of the Cold War but also, it's not seeking world domination. Nevertheless, it has become a significant power and contributor to the world's economy, its political destiny, and it will not be encroached upon, marginalized or "contained."

The neocons weren't listening. Putin became their lightning rod for ire. They have an anachronistic perception of the future. They don't make decisions like leaders living in the present. It's the mindset resurrected from the Great Depression and the Second World War years that seeks a scapegoat to blame for the failure of all one's nefarious nationalistic narratives and myths. Back then one blamed one's screw-ups on an "international Jewish conspiracy."

Today, such nationalist supremacist zealots put the yellow-star-of David blame on "an international Russian conspiracy."

In their view, a Russian-inspired peace initiative in Syria and with Iran in the autumn of 2013, compelled a pivot of neoconservative plans, away from Damascus-baiting to Maidan Square-baiting the Russian bear in 2014.

chapter three

The Great NeoCON
Of a Second Cold War

Shortly before US airstrikes would rain down on Syria in 2013, the US president stepped up to the podium at the White House and announced:

Over the last few days, we've seen some encouraging signs. In part because of the credible threat of US military action, as well as constructive talks that I had with President Putin, the Russian government has indicated a willingness to join with the international community in pushing Assad to give up his chemical weapons...

And so, to my friends on the right, I ask you to reconcile your commitment to America's military might with a failure to act when a cause is so plainly just. To my friends on the left, I ask you to reconcile your belief in freedom and dignity for all people with those images of children writhing in pain, and going still on a cold hospital floor. For sometimes resolutions and statements of condemnation are simply not enough...

America is not the world's policeman. Terrible things happen across the globe, and it is beyond our means to right every wrong. But when, with modest effort and risk, we can stop children from being gassed to death, and thereby make our own children safer over the long run, I believe we should act. That's what makes America different. That's what makes us exceptional. With humility, but with resolve, let us never lose sight of that essential truth.

Thank you. God bless you. And God bless the United States of America.

President Obama's address to the world,
Tuesday, 10 September 2013

The following day, the Russian President responded:

My working and personal relationship with President Obama is marked by growing trust. I appreciate this. I carefully studied his address to the nation on Tuesday. And I would rather disagree with a case he made on American exceptionalism, stating that the United States' policy is "what makes America different. It's what makes us exceptional." It is extremely dangerous to encourage people to see themselves as exceptional, whatever the motivation. There are big countries and small countries, rich and poor, those with long democratic traditions and those still finding their way to democracy. Their policies differ, too. We are all different, but when we ask for the Lord's blessings, we must not forget that God created us equal.

Vladimir Putin (11 September 2013)
From his *New York Times* editorial:
"A Plea for Caution From Russia:
What Putin Has to Say to Americans About Syria."

The laws of both history and geography will compel these two powers [America and Russia] *to a trial of strength, either military or in the fields of economics or ideology.*

Adolf Hitler 1945

For a nation to have an exceptional attitude it requires manufacturing a contrast. To uphold a comparison of your greatness to others, you need to project upon other people and nations their smallness or sub-humanity. America, therefore, must become hermetically sealed to criticism about being hegemonically special. All you "un-Americans," however, are special-children nations. Washington will lift you up the way Washington wants. Lesser nations commit war crimes. If necessary, America's exceptional ideas about freedom and freer markets sometimes means that it can commit "exceptional" war crimes because it has the biggest guns in town to back its taking exception to international laws for a greater and benign good.

The bald-faced arrogance of the American eagle looks down its beak from his aerie of "above-it-all" at you lesser countries that are crowding around far below, protesting exceptionalism as a negative. To the groveling prey, Big Bird USA behaves as a contradictory, even aberrantly freaky, superpower when under the spell of one of its frequent geopolitical mood swings. The American eagle with talons tightening excludes your thoughts, bars your opinions, locks out your protests, shuts out, rejects and spurns your sanctions because US might makes right—a kind of might that could at any moment be *done to you.*

When that happens, the American eagle is just too outstanding—on you, that is—for protest.

What a crock of heroic *except-crement* is this all-American form of chauvinism. It first rose to new heights of exclusion of reason in the neoconservative philosophy laid out in their evolving manifestos published in the 1990s after the end of the Cold War. American leaders took up with a straight face and a long stretch of jurisprudence, the exceptionally arrogant claim that the US Constitution protects their outrages (although it does not) to bully and contain, even destroy other nations according to our terms. Exceptional America does not "live and let live." It does not lead by its constitutional laws or by example. Anyone in hege-*money's* way is a necessary casualty of America's manifest destiny to go "abroad in search of monsters to destroy" by any monstrous atrocity it chooses. It looks the other way and lets 9-11 happen like a new Pearl Harbor, occupies Iraq on a false belief that Saddam had weapons of mass destruction, tries bombing Syria on a falsely-flagged chemical weapons attack, and ultimately aims to destroy uppity Iran on the mere rumor that it's building atomic weapons.

Don't protest so much, say the apologists. Whatever the excesses of US-exceptional actions, aren't the people of Iraq and the world "far better off and safer without Saddam Hussein in power?" Wouldn't the same be so if we found any reason, any loophole past pesky international rules and civilized laws to take down the brutal al-Assad regime, the Ayatullahs of Iran, Hezbullah? The world is better, even if America, doing the world an infernal favor, leaves a string of failed states that fester as breeding grounds for terrorists after it puts millions in the grave.

Why would American presidents like Obama, an African American and a victim of racial discrimination, sing praises of nationalistic exceptionalism when it echoes back to a discordant and ominous propaganda of a bellowing and prideful Hitler spouting the exceptionalism of the Aryan?

Take this neocon passage cited in the last chapter. Switch out and replace "America" and "Americans" with "Third Reich," "Germany" and "Aryans," etc. These neoconservative tenets sound the same in a speech, screeched by Hitler with just a slight-of-handling of a few nouns in brackets:

> *Support for* [the Third Reich's] *principles around the world can be sustained only by the continuing exertion of* [Aryan] *influence... And sometimes that means not just supporting* [German National Socialism's] *friends and gently pressuring other nations but actively pursuing policies in Iran, Cuba, or China, for instance—ultimately intended to bring about a change of regime... History also shows, however, that the* [Aryan] *people can be summoned to meet the challenges of global leadership if statesmen make the case loudly, cogently, and persistently... The alternative is to leave monsters on the loose, ravaging and pillaging to their hearts' content, as* [Germans] *stand by and watch... Because* [the Third Reich] *has the capacity to contain or destroy many of the world's monsters, most of which can be found without much searching, and because the responsibility for the peace and security of the international order rests so heavily on* [Germany's] *shoulders, a policy of sitting atop a hill and leading by example becomes in practice a policy of cowardice and dishonor. A true "conservatism of the heart" ought to emphasize both personal and* [German] *national* [socialist]

responsibility, relish the opportunity for national engagement, embrace the possibility of national greatness, and restore a sense of the heroic.

Barack Obama inspired enough American progressive voters to send him not once, but twice to Washington, yet his popularity polls among his voting base hover in the low forties to upper thirties percentile marks, similar to George W. Bush's poll numbers upon approaching the middle of his second term. Progressives complain that President Obama's record in office, especially in foreign affairs, looks and sounds—IS—a continuation of Bush's foreign policy agenda and in some ways even more neoconservative.

On April 6 2013, I wrote the following in *Predictions for 2013-2014*:

> *Since 2001, America has been in a permanent state of war ever since Congress gave G.W. Bush and all presidents succeeding him a vague and generalized carte blanche waiver to wage war against jihadists anywhere in the world and the rogue regimes who might harbor them by invoking the following nebulously defined enabling act granted to Bush:*
>
> *"That the President is authorized to use all necessary and appropriate force against those nations, organizations, or persons he determines planned, authorized, committed, or aided the terrorist attacks that occurred on September 11, 2001, or harbored such organizations or persons, in order to prevent any future acts of international terrorism against the United States by such nations, organizations or persons."*
>
> *This open-ended enabling act helped Bush unilaterally invade Afghanistan, Saddam Hussein's Iraq as it helped Obama wage an air war over Libya, land French troops into Mali, and fight robot drone wars in Yemen, Pakistan, Somalia and soon across the Western Saharan new front in this equally open-ended, tailored to be endless "War on Terror."*

*Enter Obama into the shadowy hands and inner circles
of neoconservative strategic thinking. Like other inner circles
in which he's been embraced and initiated into their powers,
he has the audacity to believe that he can change them from
within, rather than be changed by them...*

Predictions for 2013-2014,
Chapter 2: The Obama Prophecies
(Subsection: "Superfly in the Neo-Con Ointment")

US Secretary of State John Kerry seems to hold sway over his president's foreign policy decisions just like Dick Cheney had undue influence on President Bush. Detractors called Cheney Bush's Vice President "in Chief." Obama has a Secretary of State "in Chief." The Syrian chemical weapons crisis displayed at times Obama and Kerry talking at cross-purposes. Kerry vigorously and publicly rattled the cruise missile threat of airstrikes, and rejected negotiations out of hand. Then Obama stepped up to the podium at the White House, defending his military threat (and not Kerry's *Jokestergeddon* gaff) as being responsible for bringing the Syrians to talk about a diplomatic solution. He would indulge Damascus with a little of his time.

Neo-liberals playing sympathetic Obama spin-doctors, praise this inter-cabinet flip flop as his unique take on conflict resolution. Kerry had only been playing bad cop to Obama's good cop. Hence, to buy into this Pollyanna political explanation, one has to ignore the extent to which warmongering for a Syrian strike was almost unanimously rejected by US allies, Congress and over 70 percent of the American people. So, Obama consciously chose to nearly destroy his credibility as a world leader just to compel Putin to give him a diplomatic lifeline out of the political abyss he put himself in? If that's really so, I would only agree that Obama is a uniquely self-destructive "good cop."

A more troubling theory has Putin recognizing what I, and other Obama watchers, gather is his apparent lack of executive acumen. It may stem from a fatherless upbringing producing a man in the Oval

Office surrounding himself with strong alpha male father figures, like Kerry, whom he eventually cān't govern. They respectfully, reverently govern "him."

The captain is not running his ship of state. The leader is not leading, but a leading follower of cabinet members like Kerry, who is in liberal Democrat Party terms, a hubristic complement to neoconservatives in the Republican Party and the last president's Republican-neoconservative cabinet.

Kerry is also a member of the secret society of Yale, Ivy League kingmakers and power brokers called Skull and Bones, as was President G.W. Bush. Kerry is Obama's kingmaker. When he ran against Bush in 2004, it looked like a call for recounting Ohio's disputed voting might arise. Kerry quashed it, effectively surrendering victory over to his Skull and Bones opponent. In *Nostradamus and the Antichrist, Code Named: Mabus*, I put forth the following theory why:

> *Power elites in command of the Republican and Democratic Parties are the "A" and "B" teams of the same plutocratic monopoly that overlords the masses. When the A team president and congress screw up or exhaust their power cycle the influence over Americans goes to the B team presidential successor and their congressional candidates. Either way, power remains in the same hands, only the masks and outward pretenses change to trick the ignorant voters who are lulled into believing change has happened.*
>
> *Since bonesman Kerry lost to bonesman Bush, he has set up a political action committee in 2005 called Keeping America's Promise. He flooded $10 million into Democratic Party committees and the campaign coffers of 179 candidates running for US House and Senate seats, along with state and local offices in 42 states for the mid-term elections in 2006. The conspiracy minded could say bonesman B Team Captain Kerry was a major catalyst in winning a large majority in the House of Representatives and a slim majority in the Senate with the blessings and intent of his secret society to shift teams.*

Out the door of this change in masquerades steps Senator Obama who on 10 January 2008 gains his first heavyweight and very public endorsement to be president from junior Massachusetts US Senator John F. Kerry.

Kerry's endorsement preceded that of John F. Kennedy's surviving child, Caroline, and brother, the senior Mass. US Senator Edward (Ted) Kennedy.

For his efforts, Kerry had lobbied hard to be rewarded with the Secretary of State post in Obama's first term. However, that went to Hillary Clinton. He lobbied again for the job in the second term. Susan Rice, the US Ambassador to the United Nations, was Obama's first choice until she was rapidly dragged into the Benghazi embassy massacre scandal that killed the allegedly unprotected Ambassador J. Christopher Stevens and two CIA contractors in a jihad terrorist attack. Rice had appeared on US television defending the Obama administration's party line about Benghazi. As UN American Ambassador, Rice had nothing to do with State Department decisions, yet the neoconservative faction in the US Senate led by Arizona Senator John McCain (a close friend of Senator Kerry, no less) seized upon her TV appearances. Rice rapidly became the scapegoat of the Benghazi scandal and had to withdraw her bid. She was instead posted as Obama's chief NSA advisor. Kerry at last got what he coveted, rule of the State Department, and the most influential cabinet post in Obama's second term.

Progressive political watchers on liberal media outlets indulge themselves in blind-sided disbelief. They wonder rhetorically how could Obama, Kerry and other leading Democrats espouse neoconservatism.

Simple.

The lust for ultimate power is bipartisan.

Liberal leaders, like right-wing politicians, do their share of offering up their puppet strings for the pulling by captains and kings of corporate influence, the very thing President Eisenhower warned might achieve "unwarranted influence" in "the councils of government" whether "sought or unsought by the military-industrial complex."

The "potential for the disastrous rise of misplaced power exists" and persists then, as now, in the idea of American exceptionalism tied to corporate interests. It's a politician's disease and Obama has been infected by it. Why else would Obama in December 2013 acquiesce to Kerry's intention to send a political "Typhoid Mary" of neoconserva- ✓ tives to Ukraine, like Victoria Nuland, the US Assistant Secretary of State of European and Eurasian Affairs? There she prominently stood, side by side with other notable EU parliamentary leaders and (oh! there he is "again") Kerry's good friend US Senator John McCain, the latter making speeches on a podium right on Maidan Square encouraging rebellion against President Yanukovych's government.

Yanukovych was indeed just another corrupt Ukrainian oligarch who read the term "public service" as an excuse to be serviced grandly by the country's tax base. He used foreign aid to fill the pockets of his big Ukrainian business cronies and build a huge palace for himself. Nevertheless, Yanukovych had gained power through national elections in February 2010 in a political backlash to what became an ungovernable state of domestic affairs after leaders of the Orange Revolution came to power, abused it and also fell into corruption. The latter were protégés of a previous neoconservative effort during the Bush years, to manipulate a revolution in Kiev that would pull Ukraine into the European Union to eventually become a NATO ally, further tightening a ring of military and economic isolation around the Russian Federation.

Some world watchers were struck by the exceptional arrogance of a US Assistant Secretary of State and US Senator mixing with, and in McCain's case delivering speeches to, a crowd encouraging the overthrow of a troubled, albeit democratically elected government. The following question is never asked by the US mainstream media: What would Americans think if Yanukovych had sent a Ukrainian MP and his Ukrainian ambassador down to a Tea Party rally in 2010 or an Occupy Wall Street encampment in 2011 encouraging the overthrow of an unresponsive US government and a do-nothing US Congress?

Nuland's mentor, her husband Robert Kagan, is one of the found- ✓ ing fathers and influential think-tank head cases in Washington propelling the resurrection of the neoconservative movement after its disastrous setbacks in Iraq and Afghanistan under Bush. Kagan's father, Howard Kagan, is one of the original signers of the 1997 ✓Statement of Principles by the neoconservative think tank Project for the New American Century.

The standoff between Maidan demonstrators crouched behind flaming barricades constructed of cast-off tires pitted against the ranks of shield and club wielding riot police, dragged on through a frozen autumn into a frigid winter. By February, tensions came to a head. Ukraine was a national and economic basket case, ready to implode. No longer was it able to pay for Russian natural gas imports and the EU became worried its own imports might be siphoned off the Russian pipeline that transits Ukraine. Vladimir Putin's government had actively negotiated with EU counterparts for a shared aid program worth $16 billion euros from each side to keep Ukraine going through the winter of Maidan discontent. On 21 February, Russian diplomats and EU mediators, along with Maidan leaders and President Yanukovych, signed a political deal pledging to restore the Ukrainian constitution drafted during the Orange Revolution. Reforms would be completed by September 2014 with early presidential elections held no later than December 2014. It was agreed to allow the Council of Europe to stand with the opposition and investigate accusations of government corruption. The Yanukovych administration would veto the state of emergency, grant amnesty for all protestors arrested since 17 February only as long as protesters would vacate all public buildings, give up their weapons, and dismantle barricades on the Maidan Square.

Dmytro Yarosh, skin-headed leader of the ultra-nationalist "Right Sector" Party responsible for most of the violent clashes with riot police in the Maidan, rejected the agreement out of hand. On 22 February, Yarosh gathered support from other right wing elements in the mob of protesters and threatened to violently unseat Yanukovych from power. Skinheads set on fire the houses of pro-Russian parliamentarians and leaders. Right Sector thugs broke into Ukrainian Army depots and armed themselves. The police abandoned their posts guarding the Presidential Palace.

Snipers positioned on the roof of a burned out government building being used as a Right Sector's headquarters began shooting down demonstrators "and" police alike. So said Estonian foreign minister Urmas Paet in a phone conversation picked up by IBTimes with EU High Representative of the Union for Foreign Affairs and Security Policy Catherine Ashton. Paet cited surgeons working on the dozens of wounded as his sources. He later denied the opposition was involved. *Daily Beast* published video and photos implicating the Russian trained Ukrainian Security Services. *Russia Today* televised videos of Right Sector members, armed with sniper rifles, firing from the roofs. Hennaidiy Moskal, former deputy head of Ukraine's main security the SBU and the Ministry of Foreign Affairs reported in the Ukrainian newspaper *Dzerkalo Tizhnya* that "snipers received orders to shoot not only protesters, but also police forces. This was all done in order to exacerbate the conflict, in order to justify the police operation to clear Maidan."

If he's right, Yanukovych's bungled false flag incident backfired. He and other leaders of his government then escaped the country and death threats by fleeing to Russia. The opposition took up power and to this day the Interim Ukrainian government, has not begun any official investigation into the shootings that may have claimed 70 to 100 policemen and demonstrators that were shot down by snipers. One must ask, if it was Yanukovych's snipers, why not prove it? It could only legitimize their coup.

Obama demurred as neocon Nuland, McCain and neo-liberal Kerry used their influence in December 2013 to create the basis for a Western-sympathetic government in Kiev. Taped phone calls between Nuland and US Ambassador Geoffrey Pyatt two months before the Maidan coup have come to light. They clearly reveal direct US manipulation in the formation of the opposition's leadership that later became the interim government of Prime Minister Yatsenyuk. Their Ukrainian protégés came to power in late February 2014 thanks to acts of violence by neo-Nazis who broke the agreement the US State Department had helped negotiate with the EU and Russia.

Nuland had made her homecoming from Kiev in December 2013, singing the Maidan demonstrators' praises in a speech to a Ukraine-in-Washington Lobby group at the International Business Conference sponsored by Chevron Oil.

"Since the declaration of Ukrainian independence in 1991, the United States supported the Ukrainians in the development of democratic institutions and skills in promoting civil society and a good form of government—all that is necessary to achieve the objectives of Ukraine's European aspirations. We have invested more than five billion dollars to help Ukraine to achieve these and other goals…to promote Ukraine to the future it deserves."

Not all Ukrainians were on board. There were millions of ethnic Russian Ukrainians in the eastern provinces of Kharkov, Lugansk and the Donbass who felt threatened by the appointment of ultra-Ukrainian nationalists in the cabinet and parliament. The new regime's first order of business was striking the Russian language off the list of official state languages. This, along with rallies of hooded paramilitaries marching in lock-step and torch lit parades up and down the streets of Kiev chanting death to Russians, only compelled ethnic Russian provinces to form militias. Like sprouting mushrooms of early spring, barricades in squares and government buildings in the east appeared and rapidly multiplied. Eastern petitions for a referendum to vote on more autonomy from Kiev were sent to, and immediately rejected by, the Kiev parliament and interim Prime Minister. The American press was caught promoting the US State Department's big lie, that all restiveness in Ukraine's east was only a Russian-Putin "separatist" plot. Certainly Moscow had cultural, political and economic ties with Ukrainian Russians; still, evidence on the ground the Western press selectively overlooked clearly showed a popular autonomy movement was for the most part Eastern Ukrainian home grown.

Kerry visited the new Kiev government on 4 March 2014 pledging, "We will be helping." Kerry then told the crowd on Institutska Street near the Maidan barricades, "We are helping. President Obama is planning more assistance…

"It is clear that Russia has been working hard to create a pretext for being able to invade further."

Then he added a shot of something surreal aimed at Russia. To utter it, Kerry must have been selectively, even pathologically, unmindful of US outrages performed in its unilateral invasion and occupation of Iraq a little over a decade earlier.

With Iraq obviously "not" in his mind, this is what Kerry said next, "It is not appropriate to invade a country, and at the end of a barrel of a gun, dictate what you are trying to achieve. That is not 21st-century, G-8, major nation behavior."

OK, he was talking about Crimea with a population of 90-percent ethnic Russians going over to the Russians, hinting that Eastern Ukraine was next. Though his premise is disputed, there's little to dispute an inappropriate invasion of Iraq that Kerry endorsed when as a US Senator he voted in favor of giving President Bush war powers in 2002 to launch an aggressive war on, and eight-year occupation of, the people of Iraq (2003-2011). The US is a G-8 nation, but apparently American soldiers can point a barrel of a gun at Iraqis and dictate what government the Iraqis should have.

After the coup in late February, McCain, having returned from Kiev ∨ in December 2013, now pressured Congress in hearings to sign defense contracts delivering tanks and armaments to the new US-backed government that McCain rabble roused and Obama allowed Kerry to ship Nuland to Kiev to form.

Facts are ignored when they don't settle well with exceptionalism's ideologies. Yet the world ought to know why Nuland and McCain in December 2013 were caught on camera shaking hands and even haranguing the assembled revolutionaries on the Maidan alongside Oleh Tyahnybok and future Prime Minister Yatsenyuk. The former is a noted anti-Semitic, neo-Nazi head of the *Svoboda* (Freedom) Party. Svoboda dropped its former clunky-yet-politically specific title, the Social National (read National Socialist) Ukrainian Party. He and Yatsenyuk are caught together on camera in political rallies giving the audience Nazi salutes. Svoboda would go on to control, with US blessings, key cabinet posts including covering interior police security, energy and the all-important power to sell Ukraine's grain and natural gas resources to the West.

Yatsenyuk takes his orders from former Ukrainian nationalist President Yulia Tymoshenko. After the Maidan Revolution, she was released from prison serving a term for corruption by the pro-Russian, and anti-Orange, Yanukovych regime. While in prison a monitored phone conversation picked up Tymoshenko's final solution for upwards of eight million Russian Ukrainian citizens, "They must be killed with nuclear weapons!"

Other Tymoshenko apocalyptic barbs from behind bars extended that threat to Russians living beyond Ukraine's borders: "I would have found a way to kill those [Russian] assholes. I hope I will be able to get all of my connections involved…and I will use all of my means to make the entire world rise up. So there wouldn't even be a scorched field left in Russia."

Talking trash in prison? Or, does she mean it?

Like Tymoshenko, Dmytro Yarosh, the Fuehrer of Right Sector, lost his bid to become president in the 25 May 2014 election. Right Sector's largest financial patron won, the candy and chocolate confectionery manufacturing billionaire and Ukrainian oligarch, Petro Poroshenko. A number of Ukraine watchers at the time of this writing (June 2014) anticipate Poroshenko will reward Yarosh with a key security related cabinet post.

American leaders have "exceptionally" endorsed a government seeded with fascist parties openly celebrating the founding fathers of Ukrainian ultra-nationalism that actively supported the Nazi SS and Gestapo's liquidation of hundreds of thousands of Russians and Poles, along with diligently aiding in the hunt, round up and massacre of a million Ukrainian Jews during Hitler's occupation of Ukraine. History repeats itself. The CIA in the last cold war employed Nazis and other fascist elements. The same right-wing thuggery gets a second crack at Russia in a new cold war.

I predict that it will be understood later that a crisis of civil unrest in Ukraine was intended by some circles in Washington to launch a ramped up anti-Russia foreign policy in the spring of 2014. Consider what is more than a coincidence: two visits by highly placed members of Obama's cabinet. The first was on 12 April 2014, US CIA chief John Brenner came to visit Prime Minister ✓ Yatsenyuk's offices in Kiev. He met with his opposite in Ukrainian intelligence, the security minister who happens to be a member of the Svoboda Party. The following day the first military crackdown of querulous Eastern Russian Ukrainian cities started. A few days later, Right Sector's leader Yarosh moved his H.Q. from Kiev to Dnepropetrovsk, telling the press the transfer closer to the action made it easier to oversee "the liquidation of Muscovite elements" (read Ukrainian Russians).

The first delusory shooting incidents at checkpoints around the rebellious cities soon put a pause on the first crackdown. Kerry went through the motions with Russian Foreign Minister Sergey Lavrov and EU leaders in a marathon emergency meeting in Geneva on 17 April 2014 to ostensibly forestall a full-scale civil war. A truce was drafted, declaring that all militias on both sides must lay down their arms and disband. All barricades in the Maidan Square and in Russian enclaves around government buildings in the eastern provinces must be dismantled immediately. Ukrainian Russians holed up in barricaded government buildings will depart in peace. A new dialogue with all sides participating would ensue. Ukrainians could have a national debate about what kind of country they wished to live in, with peace and prosperity.

All platitudes of good will put on paper evaporated nearly as fast as the 22 February agreement. The US-backed Prime Minister Yatsenyuk immediately unraveled the deal by declaring that all heavily armed Svoboda and Right Sector militia that were roving and terrorizing the Eastern Ukraine were exceptions to the agreement. Obama, Brenner or Kerry didn't protest at all. Yatsenyuk had conveniently masked Right Sector and Svoboda's operations by designating them members of a new "National Guard." Of course, the Russian Ukrainian militias reacted by not disarming nor abandoning their barricades. That gave Kerry an opportunity to biliously condemn the separatists as further proof that Putin was calling their shots and they were pawns in a pan-Russian conspiracy to break up Ukraine, even though the Kiev fascist elements on his side broke the agreement first, just like on 22 February.

In a HogueProphecy Bulletin posted on 28 April, I wrote:

An ugly pattern repeats where EU and US leaders follow a double standard that the western media never questions as they should. It is their job to question power. The EU and US leaders say all sides should disarm, go home from occupied government buildings, and enjoy collective amnesty, but in action, only the right wing elements that violently overthrew an elected government in the first place are encouraged to keep their weapons and terrorize the other side.

The Russian Foreign Minister Lavrov had this to say about the double standard: "In Geneva we agreed that there must be total rejection of extremists and the Right Sector is still very active, and after Geneva the Right Sector staged provocations killing several people in the vicinity of Slavyansk during Easter Sunday. So nothing which was agreed in Geneva and which certainly is for the authorities in Kiev to start implementing was done by them."

Why is it, that my country that went to war to defeat Fascism and Hitler ignores this deadly hypocrisy? Is it because Ukraine has the third largest shale oil and gas reserve in Europe? Is this once again Fascism returning in our times under a new name, neoconservatism or corporate hegemony? It happened before with Hitler. Usurping resources and wealth raped from others drove much of his aims for conquest and his actions were secretly blessed by German millionaires and corporations who aimed to profit by his conquests.

The US press is echoing propaganda that Russian troops have invaded the Eastern Ukraine, that Russians manning the government buildings of a dozen Eastern Ukrainian cities are Putin's plants. Every time a new story blows with bombast out of Secretary of State John Kerry's surgically tightened lips, the facts refuting it come a day or two later. The retractions the

New York Times *publishes are conveniently crammed deep in the back pages.*

"Hear a Music Playing on the Winds of History,
Blowing Hard Once Again"
(HogueProphecy.com 28 April 2014)

On came the second visit to Kiev from an even higher US official. Five days after the falling out of the 17 April Agreement, in flew Vice President Joe Biden to Kiev. He met with Yatsenyuk on 22 April and warned that Russia faced "isolation" if it didn't stop aiding separatists in Eastern Ukraine. At the same time, President Obama in Washington ordered 600 soldiers to Poland and the Baltic states to position themselves along Russia's border.

Biden says bye bye and shortly after, on the 24th, Yatsenyuk's military launches a second Ukrainian army assault on Eastern Ukrainian provinces. The first crackdown after Brennan, and the second after Biden came to town. There was word from *Der Spiegel* that the German Intelligence Service (BND) informed the Angela Merkel government in Berlin about a private US security firm called Academi Commandos— otherwise known as the notorious "Blackwater" Agency from the US Iraqi occupation years—who had sent 400 mercenaries into Ukraine since 29 April. They would fight alongside the Ukrainian army special forces and Right Sector militias.

The shelling of cities and the massacres began in earnest. In Odessa on the Black Sea coast a month-long, peaceful demonstration comparable to an Occupy Wall Street tent camp, petitioned Kiev for a referendum allowing all Ukrainian provinces vote on whether to establish a federalist government was broken up by Right Sector elements with clubs and guns. The Odessa police obeying orders from Kiev looked on as Right Sector gangs chased the anti-Kiev protesters into the nearby House of Trade Unions. The building was set on fire by the mob heaving Molotov cocktails. Many of the protesters were burned to death. The footage is all there on YouTube to see, including thugs clubbing to death protesters who had survived jumping out of flaming windows.

The US press reported the massacre differently as merely "a fight" between pro-Ukrainian and Russian "separatist militants." A fire happened and the US press doesn't know who started it. They don't even mention the murders I saw on video, the pregnant employee working at the Trade Union, caught up in the bedlam, who was strangled by the neo-fascists. I guess if they did broadcast it, the news anchors would say, "Russian militants today happened to find themselves in a brawl. Someone started a fire and they had to jump out of windows. The fall killed them because their heads accidently fell on a man holding a club." Or, try this, you "eye-witless" news anchors: "Witnesses report that when Russian militants fell out of burning windows, the jumpers got in the way of men swinging sticks..."

Vladimir Putin on 7 May tried to lessen tension by ordering an estimated 40,000 troops back from guarding the Russian Federation's border with Ukraine. He asked ethnic Russians in the Eastern Ukrainian province to postpone their referendum and called on all parties to engage in an, "Open, honest and equal dialogue" as the only potentially rational option.

On 9 May, thousands of unarmed Eastern Ukrainians marched in their own impromptu Victory Day parades celebrating Ukraine and Russia's role in defeating Nazi Germany. In Mariupol, Ukrainian soldiers, alongside special forces of masked men in black balaclavas and uniforms, shot down dozens of these unarmed marchers. Whether these were Blackwater (Academi) mercenaries or Right Sector militia is not yet confirmed at the time of this writing. The referendum went ahead anyway with a reported 70 percent turnout. People even lined up to cast a ballot while under Ukrainian rocket and artillery fire.

The referendum was not, as the US State Department and its president in the White House or the US media called it, a "separatist vote." Ukrainians of the Donbass petitioned for the right of self-determination *within* Ukraine. President Obama and his US Secretary of State "in Chief" declared the elections illegal and a Russian provocation, even though Putin had asked that the vote not take place. From May into June, the Ukrainian Civil War was in full swing with thousands of Russian refugees flooding into Russia from Eastern Ukrainian cities under siege and constant aerial and artillery fire.

Obama in the early days of the first Russian-separatist crackdown conferred with NATO leaders in Brussels in late March coordinating tactical strategies for use against Russia. He delivered a press conference, lightly brushing off mounting cold war fears.

"This is not another cold war that we're entering into," he serenely said. "After all, unlike the Soviet Union, Russia leads no bloc of nations, no global ideology. The United States and NATO do not seek any conflict with Russia. In fact, for more than 60 years we have come together in NATO not to claim other lands but to keep nations free."

Next he visited a World War One monument to the fallen in the Battles of Ypres and Flanders Field. 2014 was the year marking a century since these battles laid waste to a generation of men. Moved by the serried ranks of stone grave markers, Obama pressed American leaders and their NATO allies commit themselves more diligently in a unified defense of Europe.

Against... Who?

"The situation in Ukraine reminds us that our freedom isn't free," said Obama.

His next foreign policy trip took place shortly after he sent Biden to Yatsenyuk, when the second Ukrainian government crackdown of eastern provinces was a few days old, and the shelling of Slavyansk, and the massacres in Odessa and Mariupol were about to take place. At that time Obama was heading in the direction of China but not like Nixon *going to China*, to arrange some great diplomatic breakthrough. Obama was visiting Asian Pacific nations "around" China on a mission to coordinate the US military with the armed forces of Japan, South Korea, Malaysia and the Philippines, speeding up the planned US military pivot out of the Middle East to face the next and future threat, the expansion of China militarily and economically in Asia.

During the week Russia celebrated the 69th anniversary of Victory Day defeating Nazi Germany, NATO amassed its allied forces in Poland and across Baltic states. They flexed their military muscle in Operation Spring Storm, the code name for the largest NATO military maneuvers held since 2003. This is the first time since the Cold War had ended in 1989 that NATO forces practiced war against Russia *right on the border with Russia.*

√ Ever since President George Bush Sr. made his pledge never to move NATO one step eastward, the US and its NATO allies have provocatively and steadily absorbed Eastern European countries and former Soviet republics right up to the Russian Federation's borders. The West's support of an anti-Russian, pro-EU putsch in Kiev on 22 February 2014 directly led to the Russian Federation acting on its threat not to tolerate any further encroachments. Wooing Ukraine westward out of Russia's sphere of influence was crossing that red line. Moscow anticipated the next step would be to turn Ukraine into a NATO ally and that would threaten Russia's strategic, Black Sea Navy harbored in the Crimean Peninsula, leased to the Russians by Kiev after Ukraine gained independence after the collapse of the Soviet Union.

Crimea, like Donetsk and Lugansk provinces, was never ethnic Ukrainian. Czarist, and later Soviet leaders, added these mostly Russian provinces for bureaucratic reasons, lobbing them into the Ukrainian SSR's jurisdiction with Crimea being the most Russian-ethnic Ukrainian of these. In March, out rushed Russian forces already stationed in Crimea to occupy the peninsula. Ninety-percent of the population welcomed them as liberators. Given the violence and atrocities committed in Eastern Ukraine, Russian nationalists in Crimea voting for secession might feel vindicated.

In reaction, the US pivots to China after the Ukrainian "feint" on Russia. NATO's next move is a military buildup to the northeast, amassing their air forces, armies and navies across the Baltic NATO allied states. Another assembly amasses to the east, along the Polish-Ukrainian border. A string of antimissile batteries are placed across the eastern frontiers of NATO ally Romania, also next door to Moldavia, a disputed breakaway province out of Russia that neighbors Ukraine.

Cynical speculation would have Ukraine become a battleground of proxies fighting and destroying each other in a "Syrian-style" civil war right along Russia's soft Ukrainian underbelly. At some point in the Russian bear baiting, Washington and military contractors hope

Putin will step into the trap and feed men and materiel into a civil war that grinds on and on, from truces to advancing tank attacks to truces broken again—a catalyst, or excuse, to tighten economic sanctions against Russia. Containment of Russia initiates a new cold war military industrial ramp up. Ukraine plays Afghanistan, a low-grade guerilla war lasting over a decade, mortally wounding the Russian bear as it did the Soviet bear in the 1980s. Regime change follows. The new "democratic" government of Russia opens itself to Western oil, gas and mineral mining. Yada, yada, yada...

Freedom lives happily ever after, Goldie Locks.

At the time of this writing, the 100th anniversary of the start of World War One (1 August 1914) is only a few months away. Today's leaders on both sides might repeat history, rendering disastrous decisions based on spotty, backwards-reasoning premises, such as what already possesses Obama in Brussels to declare there is no new cold war brewing.

Statesmen of the last Year 14 of the twentieth century (1914), likewise advanced forward into a crisis of nasty surprises because they were looking in the rear view mirror of history, defining modern warfare in archaic Napoleonic thinking of the Year 14 of the nineteenth century (1814). Beginning with the assassination of Archduke Ferdinand of Austria on 28 June 1914, a crescendo of diplomatic missteps and escalating bellicose threats exactly one month plunged the entire continent into the opening, catastrophic battles of the First World War. In four short years 30 million people were killed, European empires fell and Red Communism was on the rise. Next appeared the Black Italian and Brown Fascist revolutions of Italy and Germany. The world was utterly changed, a thousand years of political and social realities in the glowering blink of a blood-soaked eye.

On 9 November 2013, I wrote the following about 1914:

> *History's water broke 100 years ago in the year 1914...*
> *With the war fever, Europe, the dominant center of world power and economy would have its fragile surface of progress and civility scratched deeply by the bayonet of war, revealing the primal savage underneath its forward moving pretenses.*

Starting on 1 August 1914, a 1,000-year cruise of an unsinkable civilization of monarchial-ruled, world-dominating, European colonial empires stoked its boilers and surged pell-mell into the First World War, like the RMS Titanic *hitting an iceberg only two years earlier.*

The "Unsinkable" sank.

An educated hubris of empire had been programmed into the British White Star Lines CEOs and engineers who ordered and designed the Titanic. A mindless, immovable force of nature, an iceberg into which such hubris collided, took only 2.5 hours to sink the unsinkable out of sight in frigid waters off Labrador Canada on a moonless April night in 1912.

The unsinkable ship of monarchial European states that had cruised through history for 1,000 years hit the obstruction of the Great War and sank from sight relatively much faster. They capsized and sank in four brief and violently bloody years. Down went the ships of state with their bejeweled and crowned passengers. Abdicated and drowned from sight where the enduring succession of the Czars of Russia, the Kaisers of Germany, the Austro-Hungarian Emperors and the Sultans of the Ottomans along with their colonial empires in only four years, two months and 11 days! The undertow of a sinking age took many minor European kings and kingdoms down with them, leaving the post-war map of Europe choked by a plethora of political debris: new and often nationalist-oriented countries cast adrift with an uncertain political stability to keep them afloat.

Predictions for 2014, Introduction:
In the Future of 2014 are Shades of 1914 Past

In her opening statement on 6 May before the House Foreign Affairs Committee, Victoria Nuland reiterated for the record her Four Pillars of US Policy to address the challenges in Ukraine. They are a marriage model of well-known neoconservative and neo-liberal hegemonic aspirations for containing the Russian Federation and perhaps adding Russia to the 9-11 neocon hit list of candidates for regime change.

> *First, the United States is supporting Ukraine with financial, technical and non-lethal security assistance as it prepares for democratic Presidential elections on May 25th, and works to protect a peaceful, secure, prosperous and unified future for its people. Second, we are stepping up our effort to reassure our NATO allies…and we are providing support to other "front-line" states like Moldova and Georgia. Third, we are steadily raising the economic costs for Russia's occupation and illegal annexation of Crimea and its continuing efforts to destabilize eastern and southern Ukraine… And fourth, we are working with Ukraine and our European partners to leave the door open for diplomatic de-escalation should Russia change course, and make a serious effort to implement its April 17 Geneva commitments.*

Nuland's wording of what Russia needed to do to comply was a classic neocon rehash defining "negotiation" as "my way or the highway." And if you don't like it, economic worldwide sanctions will increase. The Russian economic model is seen through Nuland's rearview mirror reflection of the Soviet system pitted in a losing battle with the Free World's markets. She offered the following prediction, promising the same consequences are waiting for Russia. She laid out the groundwork for applying the new cold war's capital weapon, an economic weapon.

> *Unless Putin changes course, at some point in the not-too-distant future, the current nationalistic fever will break in Russia. When it does, it will give way to a sweaty and harsh realization of the economic costs. Then, if they are free enough to think for themselves, Russia's citizens will ask: 'What have we really achieved? Instead of funding schools, hospitals, science and prosperity at home in Russia, we have squandered*

our national wealth on adventurism, interventionism and the ambitions of a leader who cares more about empire than his own citizens'.

But it doesn't have to be this way. Russia can still step back from supporting separatism and violence and do the right thing...

The rhetorical reflections in the above betray a Freudian slip. What we hate in an enemy is often what we don't forgive lurking within ourselves. A common psychological reaction is to project our own nation's unresolved issues and faults upon our enemy. It isn't Russia. The people of the *United States* have grown weary of ruinous military adventures in Afghanistan and Iraq, hollowing out their economy by trillions of dollars. It is America blindly pledging allegiance to its exceptionalist military aggressions at the cost of neglecting to build schools and develop alternative energy sources. America's exceptional military industrial complex is draining its treasures to bolster military expenditures and interventions in place of investing in America's people, revitalizing its economy to increase employment and returning Americans back to work and prosperity.

Nuland's reflections may yet inadvertently become a fulfilled prophecy about America's future. She may unconsciously have presaged America's next revolution against its own adventurist, interventionist leadership that cares more about its own ambitions than its people.

The crisis in Ukraine affectively ends the failed neocon effort to establish "the war on terror" as the new 30-year long military-surveillance-industrial complex model for waging profitable cold war. Corporations of conflict manufacturing are stepping back to a more conservative, risk adverse business strategy. Go back to doing what you know will promise a long lasting flow of easy money. Return to the old cold war business model, like a Hollywood movie studio would. *Rocky I? Rocky II? Cold War I* pitting "Rocky" America against "Ivan" the Russian made a lot of money for a long time. Why not invest in *Cold War II?*

Pivoting to a new cold war with Russia returns the Middle East back to a tried and true secondary front status as a battleground for waging proxy wars, and as the perfect set-up for profitable theaters to supply a demand for weapons for regional arms races. All of this is intended to isolate Russia from its Syrian and Iranian partners through regime change, and finally sever all of Moscow's strategic and economic influence in the oil and natural gas rich Middle Eastern theater.

I predict these best laid plans of neo-liberal mice and neo-conmen are heading for a 1914-style nasty surprise. Nuland's dream world doesn't factor in unintended consequences. The US and EU sanctions against Russia only speed up Moscow's own long-planned pivot east to economically merge with China and to be Beijing's chief energy exporter just as it emerges as economic superpower number one in the world by mid-decade.

People who actually "listen" to Putin's vision for Russia know this is his goal. The sanctions against Russia will gravely hurt natural gas supply to the EU. America can shoulder the loss of $40 billion dollars of Russian business. Not Europe, though. The EU can't lose an annual profit of $400-billion euros doing business with Russia.

Obama speaking in Brussels cavalierly believes Russia leads nothing like a Soviet bloc of nations today. Fight this new and financial cold war and hasten a process already embarked upon by China, Russia to initiate a new geopolitical paradigm, a new bloc of nations of a North-South Axis known as the BRICS (Brazil, Russia, India, China and South Africa). They'll establish their own reserve currency, create their own petrodollar that is definitely "NOT" US minted, Mr. Obama.

Russia has a powerful geopolitical and geo-economic ally in China √ coming along for this new cold war ride. They've both been collecting huge gold reserves, Russia's has increased by 70 percent, China's by several hundred percent since 2009. Moreover, as I've been forewarning in a number of eBooks and articles, Beijing's new reserve currency, based in part on precious metals, will do the lion's share of excluding the US dollar for trade, and credit card access, and give world banks and financing markets a competitive alternative.

Wage a cold war with Russia a second time and you might witness the so-called "Free World" suffer an old-fashioned, Soviet-Union style economic implosion before 2020.

Nostradamus might have seen it coming over 450 years ago. In this passage from *Nostradamus: The War with Iran—Islamic Prophecies of the Apocalypse,* I looked at three Nostradamus verses hinting of three steps, or stumbles, the West takes waging economic warfare, perhaps beginning with sanctions over Ukraine and Crimea. The US dollar goes to war, perhaps funding a dust up with Iran, Russia's economic ally and China's chief exporter of crude oil. China and Russia retaliate with a "money bomb": an inflation explosion that makes worthless US and EU money and bonds, because the war with Iran—and by extension a new cold war with Russia and China—runs into a BRICS wall behind which is a new and competing petrol currency and reserve currency in a new banking system.

—⚏—

Stumble One: Fighting…

10 Q72
…The great King of Terror will come from the sky.
He will bring back Genghis Khan [read: a
Chinese economic superpower]
Before and after Mars [war and new enterprise] *rules happily.*

Stumble Two: Faltering…

8 Q28
The imitations of gold and silver will become inflated,
Which after the rape are thrown into the fire,
After discovering all is exhausted and dissipated by the debt,
All scripts and bonds are wiped out.

Stumble Three: Unfinanced…

7 Q25
Through long war all the forces exhausted,
So that they will not find money for the soldiers:
Instead of gold and silver, they will come to mint leather
[a metaphor for worthless money],
Gallic brass, [synecdoche for French-NATO involvement],
the crescent moon [Islam/Iran] *stamped upon it.*

—⁓—

After the Western world commanded by USA and EU suffers a greater depression than the last, an unstable global society is left behind as consequence, rife for political upheavals. It is a fertile ground for Armageddon accidentally turning a cold war with one flip of a missile switch, thermonuclear hot.

chapter four

Out of Cold War Two
Into World War Three

The blind leadeth the blind into a ditch.

Yeshua (30-33 C.E.)

One might understandably anticipate that a Ukraine divided into East and West like Germany once was would be the flint-friction Check Point Charlie of a new cold war. Start fomenting the "mind" fields of propaganda, stringing up the barbed wired minefields: NATO on the western side eyeballing, binoculars ogling, the Russians on the eastern side with their new "Warsaw Pact satellite proxies the Novi (New) Russians of the Donbass and Lugansk breakaway republics. The most likely spot for a military incident one might think unless one belongs to the world war prophets club.

Nostradamus' *Aquilon* prophecies point elsewhere. The flash point of Armageddon still lies in the biblical homeland of Armageddon.

5 Q78
The two united will not remain so for long...
They give in to a Barbare *henchman.*
There will be such a loss on both sides
That one will bless the Bark and cape of pope [Peter].

The two united are America and Russia, the Eagle kings. Line one's old French *vnis* (for *united*) may even be a Nostradamus nudge towards partially, naming the "United" States as one of the two. Unlocking the meaning of *Barbare Satrappe* linguistically unseals the riddle's secret. *Satrappe* (Satrap) is derived from the ancient Persian term for "governor of a province." Therefore he is a subordinate "ruler" to the Persian Shah (Emperor). He does the higher power's bidding ruling a province inside the greater sphere of influence of a Persian empire. The secondary definition of Satrap, given by *Merriam Webster Dictionary*, is "subordinate official" or "henchman." That could further imply he's a proxy, or a vassal, in this case perhaps of modern-day Iran (Persia).

Barbare is Nostradamus' word specifically used to describe the Muslim terrorists of his day, the Barbary Pirates or Corsairs who often hijacked ships, raided and terrorized the Mediterranean coast of France in the sixteenth century as chief "vassal" of the Ottoman Empire. These pirate terrorists posed the greatest threat to Western Christendom during Nostradamus' lifetime as vassals of Sultan Suleiman the Magnificent at the high water mark of Ottoman expansion into Eastern Europe and the Western Mediterranean region.

The Barbary Corsairs anchored their pirate ships in ports along the North African coast of what are present-day Morocco, Algeria, Tunisia and Tripoli (modern-day Libya). It's more than likely Nostradamus used a contemporary metaphor—Muslim pirates as terrorists—to describe Muslim terrorists hijacking planes and raiding or blowing things up in his distant future, our present time.

With this said, an attempt to forge a unity and friendship between Russia and America is undermined; it is severed by the act of an Islamic terrorist, either a proxy or henchman of Iran, or, a North African or Arab henchman allied to either the US or the Russians. He's employed as a proxy point man in a wider strategic struggle between the two, perhaps in a renewed cold war.

Why specifically an "Arab"?

Look deeper into *Barbare* as a hidden anagram. Simply follow Nostradamus' enigma decoding rules. In this case, they allow us one redundant letter *r* either dropped entirely or replaced:

barba(r)*e*

Next, reverse the first *b* to create a *d*. Move the second *a* after the remaining *r*:

darabe

Punctuate and capitalize:

d'Arabe

The English translation of Nostradamus' prophecy would now read:

5 Q78
The two united will not remain so for long...
They give in to <u>an Arab</u> henchman.

Whose henchmen is it? If Iran, then it could be the Shi'ite government currently in power in Iraq; and/or, Iran's main ally in the region, the Shi'ite Alawite Bashar al-Assad of Syria, who is currently waging a civil war with Syrian Sunni Muslim rebels. Assad utilizes Southern Lebanon's Shi'ite Hezbullah forces in that fight. At the time of this writing, Assad's regime is gradually winning the civil war. The leaders of Hezbullah are satrapy henchmen to Syria "and" Iran, for it is through Hezbullah that Iran can wage proxy wars, such as in 2006, against America's chief proxy (henchman) in the Middle East, Israel. The Russian Federation identifies Assad's Syria as its remaining Soviet era ally in the Middle East. Saddam Hussein's Iraq, along with Egypt and Yemen, all had been Soviet proxies or "henchmen" during the last cold war as was Libya (the modern *Barbare*-Barbary Coast pirates). The neoconservatives with the help of Obama's neo-liberal supremacists have crossed the last two proxy regimes off their list, leaving Assad's Syria next. Russia is not an ally of Iran in an official sense, yet economic ties are drawing them close and sometimes Russia is a source supplier of weapons systems for Tehran.

The fate of the Syrian al-Assad dictatorship could be the cause of the final breakdown globally of any unity of purpose for the US and Russia. Soon after, it unexpectedly leads to a new cold war flaring thermonuclear hot. To know why this is a present-day or near future event depends on the right interpretation of the final two lines of this quatrain:

5 Q78

The two united will not remain so for long…
They give in to an Arab henchman.
There will be such a loss on both sides
That one will bless the barque and cape of pope [Peter].

The *barque* (bark), a small boat with a cross standing at the prow, is the sign of the Catholic Holy See, the Vatican "ship" of state. It symbolizes the fishing bark of St. Peter, first Bishop of Rome and the first Pope. Prophecies of the Irish medieval St. Malachy and Catholic prophet Nostradamus share a similar vision of the final pope being either directly named or possessing the symbols or signs within a family coat of arms of Peter the Fisherman. Vatican papal conventions prevent a future pope ever being named Pope Peter. Only the first Bishop of Rome, St. Peter, can call himself Peter. Then again, a pope's Christian name could be Peter. Take for instance the current Pope Francis.

Cardinal Bergoglio named himself after St. Francis of Assisi whose Christian name was Francesco di *Pietro* (Peter) di Bernardone. The 112 cryptic Latin phrases comprising the prophecy of St. Malachy can hide a future pope's birth name or his new name as a pontiff. The 112th pope on the list is called *Petrus Romanus* (Peter of Rome). He is the final pope before Judgment Day. Francis is that last pope on the list. Peter of Rome can be Pope Francis because St. Francis was also called "Peter."

This Peter, to whom one "blesses the barque" in Nostradamus' quatrain is a contemporary of the Arab henchmen who undermine peaceful unity between America and Russia *in our times* resulting in a war of great loss on both sides. Nostradamus is possibly trying to describe the hundreds of millions of Americans and Russians extinguished from a nuclear exchange between two nations holding 90 percent of the atomic and thermonuclear weapons on the planet.

The Syrian Civil War is also mentioned in a verse about the 9-11 terror attacks, because, as we will see, *Arethusa* is a classical name for a modern Syrian stronghold fighting against the Assad regime:

1 Q87

Earth shaking fire of Neptune from the center of the Earth.
Will cause the towers around the New City to shake:
Two great rocks for a long time will make war,
And then Arethusa shall color a new river red.

Follow the classical metaphors: Neptune is God of the oceans "and" earthquakes. A natural temblor is implied yet Nostradamus the sixteenth-century poet might try to describe the unheard of explosive might of conventional artillery reverberating back from distant future times, peppering and shaking down the buildings of many Syrian cities like a great quake. Even the five-to-ten story tenements of Damascus, Homs, and Aleppo would appear to Nostradamus as great towers shaken by artillery fire.

Images in Nostradamus' mind often blend together, piling up more than one event or crowding together several persons mistaking them as one, especially if there's some relationship, some karmic action and reaction between them. For instance, Nostradamus' quatrains mistake the German invasion of France in the twentieth century as one invasion, not two (1914 and 1940), because he melds accurate details of both German advances from separate world wars. One therefore can't rule out a phrase bridge to the famous "9-11" quatrains—6 Q97 and 10 Q49:

At forty-five degrees latitude, the sky will burn,
Fire approaches the great _new city_,
Immediately a huge, scattered flame leaps up,
When they want to have verification from the Normans [French].

> *Garden of the world near the <u>new city</u>,*
> *In the path of the hollow mountains* [read, <u>towers</u>] *:*
> *It will be seized and plunged into the boiling caldron,*
> *Drinking by force the waters poisoned by sulfur.*

Nostradamus builds his word bridges with double entendre. The "new city" (New York) and its "hollow mountains" (towers) shaking and falling into the "boiling cauldron" of their own debris fields, as if in an earthquake, may be somehow tied to the towers of Syrian cities shaken down years later by artillery fire out of the blue. When "the sky will burn" with fireballs hitting the two towers of the World Trade Center in New York, they do so because Islamic terrorist hijacked jets made into missiles, hitting both structures at 45-degree angles the day after French intelligence officers tried to warn their US opposites in Washington that the attack was coming. A decade later, over in Syria, once again Islamic terrorists contribute their infernal part delivering fire from the skies over Assad-held Damascus, and other Syrian cities, where "scattered flames leap up." The same French who tried to warn the US on 11 September 2001 of the Islamic terror attack, also once ruled Syria as a colony and they are the most willing NATO nation to get militarily involved in America's adventures in Libya (2011-2012) and Syria (2013). That could be how Nostradamus intended his double entrendres to span together karmic reoccurrences in future history.

Back to 1 Q87. The seismic metaphors move from the literal to the metaphorical. The *two great rocks* could be Russia and the US, engaged in a standoff. The tensions, "fault lines," suddenly break and shake in a renewed cold-war struggle. Or, it's the fault lines of tension between US-Russian proxies.

Why this is possible is explained by the meaning of *Arethusa*. She's the classical Greek nymph who in legend changed herself into a spring. By calling Arethusa *red*, Nostradamus warns us of lava flows in a double entendre of quaking war and a river running red with blood, a river whose name is specifically hidden in the classical metaphor *Arethusa*, the ancient name of a town in the rebellious Sunni heartland of the civil war. Four years before the civil war commenced shaking down Syrian towns and cities, I wrote in 2007:

There is a Syrian connection to the classical town named after the goddess Arethusa. She is not only the goddess of volcanoes (earth-shaking fire) but possibly used to name modern day Ar Rastan. It was once an Ancient Roman settlement along the Orontes (Asi) River just inland from the Syrian Mediterranean coast, between Himms [Homs] and Hamah. The Asi River running red with blood is one of Nostradamus' stark stabs at poetry about a future battleground along northern Syrian approaches to Lebanon and the Bekaa Valley—one of the principle routes Syria uses to supply Hezbullah. This could be Nostradamus' description of Israeli air and missile attacks on the road to Lebanon, or ports along the nearby coastline where Syria has its only access to the sea. (Nostradamus: The War with Iran First edition, May 2007)

Israel has indeed launched major airstrikes into Syria (January and May 2013) in hope of eliminating the chemical weapons it believed the Syrian regime was secretly shipping on supply routes into the Hezbullah-held Bekaa Valley.

In February 2012, roughly a year into the Syrian Civil War, I wrote a dire forecast about an unending civil war destroying the country. Sadly, two years later, at the time of this writing, the passage sounds like it was written yesterday:

Fault lines of of another kind have gripped, tugged and built up sectarian tensions in Homs, Hamah and Ar Rastan—all strongholds of the Sunni majority, which the al-Assad regime (consisting mostly of the Shia Alawite minority and Syrian Christians) has tried over the past half century to dilute with a steady influx of Alawites. Now the two great rocks of Shia and Sunni Muslim dogma "make war" along the Orontes.

And that river runs through it all—metaphorically speaking. It runs red. Not with lava but the spilled blood of thousands yet to be slaughtered as Syria descends into full-scale urban civil war. Think Beirut. Think Lebanon in the 1970s. Not one city shattered by street fighting but a dozen.

This apocalyptic potential if actualized may spread and unhinge a volatile region, just when brinksmanship between Israel and the US with Iran has escalated to levels of severity and threat not seen since 2005–2007. As stated earlier, the cities on the Orontes now under fire are the main supply routes for Iran's allies in Lebanon taking aim at Northern Israel with 20,000 rockets. There may be one more interpretive layer hidden in 1 Q87 that takes us from Syria and returns us to Iran. First let us review the prophecy:

1 Q87

Earth shaking fire of Neptune from the center of the Earth.
Will cause the towers around the New City to shake:
Two great rocks for a long time will make war,
And then Arethusa shall color a new river red.

This time the rocks of tension are Judeo-Christian (US and Israel) versus Muslim Syria allied to Islamic theocratic Iran. I view the following as a picture published in 2007 that better comes to us as a shadowy, chilling potential for war when astrology prophecies of Nostradamus once again frame these bellicose potential events in future time: 2015 or 2016:

"This could foretell the seismic quake of Israeli tactical nuclear weapons drilling deep into Iranian underground nuclear installations at Arak, Natanz and Esfahan [Iran]. Nostradamus either gives an allusion to a new terrorist attack on New York as consequence to a war with Iran, or it is foreseen here accidentally or purposefully out of time sequence—the new city is New York. It shakes with the attack on 11 September 2001. In other prophecies (6 Q97 and 10 Q49) Nostradamus describes the latitude of New York, and the collapse of what he

calls great "hollow mountains" that are "plunged into the boiling cauldron" of their own fiery debris. The acts therefore are reversed in his mind. The towers shook and then the earthshaking of Iran as consequence. The two rocks, figuratively speaking are Syria and Israel. If it is about Iran then expect their Syrian ally pulled into the fight. This war will be far worse than all others Syrians fought with Israel." (Nostradamus: The War with Iran, First edition, May 2007)

Nostradamus Syria Predictions
Hogueprophecy Bulletin
(17 February 2012)

The Middle East is the fire trap set by *barbare* henchmen that attracts their American and Russians masters like moths to the immolation in a Third World War. The US and USSR nearly came to direct blows over the Six Day War (1967) and again, as Arab (Soviet) and Israeli (US) proxies brawled in the Yom Kippur War of 1973. Syria in the past played a key military role in both wars. It does so again in the new cold war, becoming an Arab flashpoint, only this time not as a fellow Soviet ally with Egypt, but as Satrap of Russia's neighbor and new regional associate, Iran.

Just when could these moths touch flame?

Nostradamus' many prophecies about war between Iran and Western powers disclose dates, names of combatants and theaters of battle centuries before they happened.

5 Q25
The Arab Prince, Mars, the Sun, Venus [in] *Leo,*
The rule of the Church will succumb [surrender] *to the sea…*

The Arab Prince could be Saddam Hussein. He is mentioned as such, though it could yet apply to an important player in the oncoming war, a present or future King of Saudi Arabia. At the time of this writing (May 2014) King Abdullah is secretly conspiring to integrate his military with the Israelis so that Zion's surprise attack over Saudi airspace might pass across the Persian Gulf, striking targets harboring Iran's supposed nuclear weapons program, if indeed they have one. The timeframe for all of this is bracketed by previous- and near-future conjunctions of Mars, the Sun and Venus in Leo. The last took place in August 2000 (the turn of the Christian Millennium or *rule of the Church*). The future conjunction lands in August 2015, a month before Mars in Leo will become "equally fiery" with Saturn entering Sagittarius in September 2015 as related in the following prophecy:

4 Q67
In the year when Saturn and Mars are equally fiery,
The air is very dry, a long comet [missile?]*:*
From hidden fires a great place burns with heat,
Little rain, hot wind, wars and raids.

We therefore have a convergence of conjoining planets for war just as history passes out of the final degrees of the Mayan Orb ending the time of death and renewal of a 5,000-year Mayan epoch in 2016. This is the time when the grand alignment of the Earth, Sun with Galactic Center began its 30-year astrological influence beginning in 1986 peaking between the winter solstices of 21 December 1998 and 1999, with its cosmic impact continuing until winter solstice, 21 December 2016.

The "air is very dry" in the Middle East, made more so by increased global temperature rises from climate change. The worst drought in the Levant in modern record was a major cause of Syria's civil war.

The long comet is a missile. The "hidden fires" are the explosion of bunker buster bombs digging deep through the earth to detonate inside underground Iranian nuclear installations. They burn with the heat of thermobaric-pressurized blasts. *Little rain* in Iran, suffering climate change droughts like Syria and *hot winds, wars and raids* over the Persian Gulf.

Will the Peacemakers be given a chance to alter this scenario? Prophecies full of cryptic nuances tend to gain more clarity as the times they frame approach the present. This is possible because we solve a riddle through recognizing details unique to our times. People of bygone days can't conceive what we know and experience in our times. For instance, the references to Geneva in Nostradamus' prophecies understandably had interpreters before modern times link them—and not with much satisfaction—to what had been the breeding ground of French Protestantism in Nostradamus' day, sixteenth-century Geneva, where Jean Calvin and his Calvinists dwelled.

After the First World War, Geneva became the capital of the new League of Nations. At the close of the Second World War, it became the second capital of the United Nations. Thus men gathering in Geneva took on a more workable role as negotiators waging peace. Indeed the first stop for Ronald Reagan meeting Mikhail Gorbachev on the road to ending the first cold war was Geneva.

Put that new information into play: two verses might tell us if a civil war in Syria can be settled politically, or if peace initiatives between America and Iran over Iran's nuclear program held in regular meetings of both diplomatic missions in Geneva, starting in 2014, ever had a chance.

1 Q47

The speeches of Lake Leman [Geneva] *become angered,*
The days drag out into weeks,
Then months, then years, then will fail,
The Authorities will damn their useless powers

9 Q44

Leave, leave Geneva everyone!
Saturn will change wealth to weapons,
Those against RAYPOZ will be exterminated.
Before the invasion, the heavens will show signs.

Line two of 9 Q44 is an important astrological dating. Saturn will complete its intensely karmic transit through Scorpio by the end of December 2014, and then punctuate it with a three-month encore in Scorpio in the summer of 2015. It takes Saturn roughly 28 years to orbit the 12 signs of the Zodiac, thus returning to a new pass through Scorpio for a transit of a little more than two years. Saturn is symbolized in astrology as the Grim Reaper, or ruler of reality checks confronting our limitations. During its transit through Scorpio, the world in general, and especially nations with Saturn factoring prominently in their birth charts, must review the past 28 years of successes and mistakes in the realm of financial institutions, monetary reserve currencies and banking. A wise nation under Saturn's Scorpionic passing plans ahead for the next cycle of 28 years considering what it wishes to leave as an inheritance to the next generation. Nations defining or reinventing their viewpoint on economics and financing should learn from their mistakes of the past 28 years and prosper; whereas, those nations holding onto their self-limiting views and political-economic dogmas suffer 28 years of crisis and disaster. Saturn in Scorpio is about a process of transition, a kind of death to the old to clear the way for new ideas and a new life for the nation.

The Scorpio Saturn transit directly impacts the future of the United States because it passes over the US Ascendant at eight degrees Scorpio every 28 years, directly triggering a time for self-reflection and re-invention (something Americans can do amazingly well), bringing positive change. On the other hand, if the opportunity of reinvention is missed or botched, expect exceptionalism's continuation of mistakes in the nation's outer expression, its economic, domestic and foreign policies, etc.

The sign of Scorpio is ruled by Pluto, which has dominion over atomic power (plutonium). America was the first nation to penetrate deep into what lies underneath matter, split the atom and create a nuclear bomb. America ever enjoys being first among nations: in this case, the first to use nuclear weapons. The karmic consequences of the right use or abuse of this ultimate power in the next Saturn cycle will be set in motion by decisions actualized or not ventured during the current transit (2012-2014 and summer 2015).

Given the very negative thrust of these two Geneva verses, Saturn's forecast about finances and economics in the next 28 years do not look good. The intolerant may trump the peacemakers of Geneva, they may soon find a new reason for continuing a renewed cold-war oriented military industry. In *Nostradamus: The War with Iran*, I explained how RAYPOZ could be an anagram for an experimental nuclear reactor built by the French for Saddam Hussein outside of Baghdad in the early 1980s called OSIRAK. The French technicians were word playing with the name of the Egyptian god of death, Osiris, linking it to the French spelling of Iraq (IRAK). If we enlarge the scope of this enigmatic word RAYPOZ, it stands for Iraq, Iran, or the aspirations of the Islamic world in general, to create a nuclear "Islamic" atomic or thermonuclear bomb.

RAYPOZ can, by extension, stand for the ancient Persian Zopyros. He betrayed Babylon (Iraq) to the Persians (Iran). At the moment, Iraq is poised to break up in a second civil war in part because its Shi'ite dominated, pro-Iranian government under Nuri al-Maliki has persecuted Iraq's Sunni minority. Al-Maliki plays Zopyros, betraying Iraq's future as a contiguous nation.

Any NATO effort to get directly, militarily involved in the Syrian Civil War to fulfill a neocon and Israeli strategic plan to isolate Iran from its Arab allies before directly striking it, no later than the mid-2010s, somehow goes terribly wrong. America's proxies drag them into a direct, perhaps even nuclear, conflict with Russia, a friend and ally of both Syria and Iran. China depends on Iran as its chief oil exporter to feed an insatiable energy demand.

The heavens "have" shown signs of these approaching dangers.

First off, the current transit of Saturn in Scorpio not only crosses over the eight-degree Ascendant of the US, Saturn passes over the Natal Sun sign of the European Union, which is also eight degrees Scorpio! Time is running out for both America and the EU. Reinvent yourselves. Time to stop conjuring up a past-oriented, though new, cold war before the 28 years of karmic and atomic consequences begin after the end of the transit in September 2015.

Another portent the heavens showed the world happened on 20 April 2014, the day Easter and anniversary of Adolf Hitler's birthday came together on that year's calendar. There appeared a rare grand-cross squaring of Mars in Libra, Jupiter in Cancer, with Pluto in Capricorn, hooked in a near 90-degree uppercut with Uranus grappling once again with a notorious return of a lingering square. In layman's terms, leaders of the world would be grandly cross, executing blind decisions at cross-purposes to reasoning out a more harmonious human future. It must be remembered that under this darkest of malefic squares, leaders of the US and NATO backed the fascist-infested interim Ukrainian government. They goaded them to wage a full military and skin-headed militia-led crackdown on the Eastern Ukrainian Russian provinces, spawning a civil war. One might even prophesy a vision of historians looking back at late April 2014 as the time a new cold war was born in the Ukrainian Crisis.

Those against RAYPOZ are the Western powers, the US and NATO. The Ukraine troubles will cause a blow back to Iran. Even if it actually was pursuing nuclear weapons' capability, Iran has no capacity to annihilate the Western powers, but cornering Russia, Iran's ally, mindlessly amplifies tensions in the Middle East parallel to NATO's encroachment of Russia's western frontiers. Incidents on both fronts could cause a nuclear war exterminating the enemies of RAYPOZ. The spread of a sectarian Islamic civil war out of Syria into Iraq on the new cold war's Middle Eastern front could also lead to an unanticipated incident precipitating a US-Russian military crisis that sends the peacemakers running for their lives from Geneva.

Where they run is wide eyed into these catastrophes of the prophecies listed below.

The expanded donor's edition of this book will be published on 25 July; however, the international edition will appear on 1 August 2014, the centenary anniversary of Stormberger's first prophecy that is among the most clear ever recorded for posterity. We now wait for what wickedness might issue down the iron track of time beyond the year 2014.

And after the second great war between the nations will come a third universal conflagration, which will determine everything. There will be entirely new weapons. In one day more men will die than in all previous wars combined. Battles will be fought with artificial weapons. Gigantic catastrophes will occur.

Stormberger's catastrophes might include something planetary as well as thermonuclear. He adds his voice to other prophets trying to uncover the future's deadly doomsday riddle such as Nostradamus in his Mabus and 27-Year War of the Third Antichrist prophecies.

Nostradamus foresaw three Antichrists, their real names are hidden in anagram codes. The first, *PAU NAY LORON*, is NAPAULON ROY (King Napoleon). The second is *Hister* (Adolf *Hitler*). The third Antichrist, code named *Mabus*, currently has four top contemporary candidates, two from the West, two from the Middle East, all four karmically entwined, drawn into the lands of the *barbare* in a struggle for Judeo-Christian or Islamic supremacy over the Middle East. The first is Saddam Hussein of Iraq. Next is Osama (Usama) bin Laden, the dean of Jihad terrorism taught at his university of "al-Qaeda" (the Front) in Afghanistan. He's responsible for planning and inspiring the 9-11 attacks that inadvertently handed the neocons the Cold War on Terror guided by the last two top candidates, Presidents G.W. Bush and Barack Obama. The Ukraine crisis broadens the scope of the new cold war between the US and its NATO allies against Russia and its allies the Syrians, Iranians and the Chinese. Though Obama, at the time of this writing, is the last living candidate still wielding power, the fate foretold by Nostradamus for his third and final antichrist pins his 27-year war on the aftermath and consequence of the Third Antichrist's annihilation. Unlike Napoleon and Hitler, he is the first to fall in this Third World War of terror.

2 Q62

Mabus very soon then will die, [then] *will come,*
A horrible undoing of people and animals,
At once one will see vengeance,
One hundred powers, thirst, famine, when the comet will run.

When this Mabus dies, there will be a great vengeance of 100 nations going to war at a time of increased thirst (global warming droughts) and global famine's advent when a comet (falling nuclear missile?) will run through the skies. What isn't clear is whether the death of

Mabus causes the horrible undoing of people and animals; or, vice versa.

Nostradamus seems to be scratching his head. He's penned words as vague as Stormberger's, who we recall didn't specify exactly what his "gigantic catastrophes" actually are. Are they natural, bellicose, or both? Is our world unraveled by a nuclear war or is Nostradamus' *undoing of people and animals* in some way a reference to nuclear war *and* global warming happening at the same time, driving the Earth out of ecological balance in a double-edged planetary climate disaster?

Does one beget the other? A habitable human and animal climate undone by atomic blasts? On the other hand, is the tension of climate change bringing intolerable strain to bear on fragile systems sustaining human global economics and thus bringing civilization to a point of collapse, causing the war of the antichrist?

Delving deeper into the linguistics of 2 Q62's second line, I wrote in 2008:

> *The killing of Mabus is followed afterwards by* a horrible undoing of people and animals.
>
> *This phrase is significant and unique in all of Nostradamus' lurid and violent visions. This "undoing" is huge. Global. The old French for "undoing" (defaite) incorporates an event that* undoes, unmakes, unravels *the world of people and animals. It implies a dramatic, sudden and catastrophic defeat, a rout, an eclipse of an age—it decries the fall of shadows over civilization due to the death of Mabus. The horrible undoing is a great wasting, an obscuring of reason, something fundamentally embarrassing to what was perceived as reality, truth, moral, or human before Mabus fell.* Defaite *implies something that emaciates, discomposes civil order and perhaps even unravels the climate and ecological balance, leading to a threat of extinction that in a worst-case scenario decimates the world of people and animals.*
>
> *There might be coming a destruction of people and animals that begins as a military incident or war comes from an*

ecological disaster and/or global famine and droughts. Or the unraveling has a social-economic trigger, such as the collapse of one or many supersystems that keep our global society functioning. Futurist Roberto Vacca coined and defined the word supersystem *as super-organizations sustained by machines and single energy sources. For instance, our fossil fuel based oil and coal-fired civilization uses the petrochemical supersystem. Agriculture is another system, as is transportation of goods by air, land and sea.*

Nostradamus and the Antichrist, Code Named: Mabus
(First Edition, September 2008)

The Hopi, like other Native American prophetic traditions, lean decidedly towards war born out of upended nature. Their visions parallel many of Nostradamus' prophecies about famine, drought, rising oceans aided by a "fire in the sky," implying planetary climate change decidedly disrupts civilized and natural life on Earth.

What the catastrophes are may be unspecified, yet Stormberger is clear about the state of unawareness in which humanity enters into them:

With open eyes will the people of the Earth enter into these catastrophes. They shall not be aware of what is happening, and those who will know and tell, will be silenced. Everything will become different than before, and in many places, the Earth will be a great cemetery. The third great war will be the end of many nations.

Are we not now confronted with a majority of people either blissfully ignorant or openly—even righteously—uninformed by their politicians about the mountainous scientific data proving global warming is human manufactured?

Those who tell are thousands of scientists around the world stymied by your news media, your political leaders and the climate-change denying fossil fuel corporations. The latter lobby hard to have overview reports that are sent to legislators watered down. They even spend tens of millions of dollars on smear campaigns to discredit and silence solid evidence even while 97.5 percent of the Earth's scientists conclude that global warming is an oncoming human-made planetary disaster.

Are any of you reading this aware of leaked secret reports in 2010 coming from the CIA concluding that climate change will foster climate "wars" as the next and number one national security challenge for the US? The natural world's war—or the next world war, even—the CIA anticipates can hasten civilization's breakdown in a plague of conflicts. It isn't World War "Three" per se. Rather, it might be more like what I had predicted and published in *The Millennium Book of Prophecy* 14 years before the CIA wrote their report on the same theme.

It's not World War Three. It's a World War "Free-for-All."

I defined the Third World War caused by climate change as not one but upwards of 70-to-100 conflicts raging across the planet. Half of these range from being internal revolutions to civil wars, all boiling over chaotically as if a heat-waved world fanned a demonic possession, a collective madness to destroy everything. The heat stroke of a feverish atmosphere drives populations into a life-and-death gamble to seize and horde dwindling resources of a broken experiment in the spiritual and intellectual uplifting of human consciousness out of the habits of primeval savagery. If this worst-case fiction scenario becomes the future's fact, we enter the next, very "hot" Dark Ages, and put back civilization's evolution 500 years.

The Austrian monk from the thirteenth century, Johann Friede, also indicates climate change and other natural disasters are a significant catalyst for the unraveling of the world of animals and humans in a kind of ecological Judgment Day.

When the great time will come, in which mankind will face its last, hard trial, it will be foreshadowed by striking changes in nature. The alteration between cold and heat will become more intensive, storms will have more catastrophic effects, earthquakes will destroy greater regions and the seas will overflow many lowlands. Not all of it will be the result of natural causes, but mankind will penetrate into the bowels of the earth and will reach into the clouds, gambling with its own existence. Before the powers of destruction will succeed in their design the universe will be thrown into disorder, and the age of iron [the industrial, technological age?] *will plunge into nothingness.*

Are we not living in these times now? Look out your window at the extremes of weather. Note in a mere dozen years passing the striking retreat of our mountain glaciers and the shrinking of Earth's polar ice cap. In the US the superstorms of winter simply morph into the violent tornado outbreaks and straight-line thunder windstorms of spring and monsoon-like thunderstorms of summer. Smell the mega fires in the flinty air from sustained mega droughts. Witness, will you, on YouTube the uncensored, real time record of the ocean spilling over its banks like a river in flood into the cities and fishing villages of the northeastern Honshu coast of Japan in the Tohoku quake and tsunami of March 2011. Consider the Indian Ocean tsunami of December 2004 overflowing lowlands and coasts of Sumatra, Thailand, Sri Lanka, India, even distant Somalia, then retreating with the corpses of a quarter million people taken out to sea.

Not all of these quakes are natural. Consider the fracking wells drilling deep into the crust of the Earth causing earthquakes where none took place before. Regard the specter clouds of the evil spirits belching from smokestack and car muffler, penetrating beyond the clouds to trap solar rays in the atmosphere like a greenhouse heating up your world.

Your glaciers will go on melting. Oceans will rise, exerting pressures on the subduction zone fault lines off your ocean shores, pressing water down on them, the added weight unleashing more superquakes and tsunamis upon you.

Is this not what all of us are making, this new abnormal existence? We are all using the greenhouse gases to power our machines and modernize our lives in a planetary gamble. Our blue planet in space is a casino chip on destiny's crap table and we're throwing snake eyes. Centuries ago Johann Friede apparently visualized us doing it, undermining the world of people and animals like Nostradamus said. We are walking with open eyes into these great catastrophes as Stormberger warned.

Where there's a manmade climate change, there are first economic, then political and at last military consequences. War is poised to pounce on the ignorant, unawares, just around the corner of present times. To help humanity step away from this terrible course may depend on a hopeful rekindling of friendship between America and an emerging Russian Federation. Hegemonic interests aim to sabotage this potential future.

Some of you watch it happening and you blink.

You postpone pressuring your press to tell the news straight. You wait for some other fellow to lobby your leaders, demanding they give peaceful negotiation a chance of resolving troubles in Ukraine, Syria, Iran or any other new cold war flash point. As we go on sowing blindness and denial, rather than positively act, so shall we reap a night of death for human civilization foreseen by Nostradamus.

Let this not happen:

5 Q8

There will be let loose living fire and hidden death.
Horror inside dreadful globes.
By night the city will be reduced to dust by the fleet.
The city on fire, helpful to the enemy.

2 Q91

At sunrise one will see a great fire.
Noise and light extending towards [Aquilon-Eagle kings]
of the North.
Within the earth death and cries are heard.
Death awaiting them through weapons, fire and famine.

The living fire of the Sun, the human-invented Sun-fire of thermonuclear weapons, detonate and leave behind in the smoking darkness a hidden death of radiation fallout to sicken and kill all those left unskeletonized by atomic fire. Nostradamus has looked deep into our future and seen underneath the casing of atomic weapons the dreadful spherical-shaped atomic-bomb triggering device of a fusion warhead. These *dreadful globes* can turn a city into glowing, radioactive dust.

Nostradamus furthermore seems to be aware of nuclear war targeting protocols. The first missiles fired by Russia and America from their silos, submarines, or strategic bombers, fall like Nostradamus' running comet striking the southernmost targets then spreading their mini-Sun fireballs in a carpet-bombing pattern advancing northwards. Nostradamus hears our lament and death rattle while cloistered in the darkness of bomb shelters. Death waits to claim billions of us first through atomic weapons and radioactive firestorms destroying our cities, then follows the famine.

It is famine, more than fallout or blast effects that will kill the vast majority of us in a thermonuclear war. When thousands of ports and cities go up in nuclear flame and smoke, not only are the means to grow food and transport foodstuffs destroyed but the dust and smoke sent into the stratosphere by nuclear detonations could block out the Sun's rays from 18 months to two years in a "Nuclear Winter." Crops feeding humanity will starve of sunlight and warmth. Most of you will starve and wither away like them.

Another Austrian seer, calling herself Madame Sylvia, foresaw this nuclear winter. She wrote the following for prophetic posterity, sounding the alarm before she died in 1948, the same year the Berlin blockade officially started the last cold war. Her "fallen colossi" in this horrible vision have long been mistaken for the USSR and US. This event is still waiting in the future:

Frenzy, folly and madness… Two corpses by the roadside, two fallen colossi [United States and the Russian Federation?] *terrible struggle, lament, wreck, ruin and smoke. Where is the Sun? Where is day? Where is God and his help? Everything is dark on Earth. Hell has opened its gates.*

Three hundred years earlier Pastor Bartholomaeus continues the "fallen Colossi" theme:

Neither of the two adversaries will conquer nor be vanquished. Both mighty ones [Russia and America?] *will lie on the ground.*

Viking seers, circa 900 C.E., composing the Norse Eddas, record a tale of Viking Armageddon known as Ragnarök giving us the duration of Nuclear Winter written over 740 years before Bartholomaeus' prediction:

Heavy snows are driven and fall from the world's four corners. The murdering frost prevails. The Sun darkened at noon. It sheds no gladness. Devouring tempests bellow and never end. Men wait for the coming of summer in vain. Twice winter follows winter over the world, which is snow-smitten, frost-fettered and chained in ice.

Once the nuclear winter subsides, the Sun and warmth will emerge again loaded with lethal rays further killing crops and blinding eyes with cataracts. The Sun will shine cancer down on the survivors because atomic detonations have perforated the protective ozone layer to the extent that it will take a century or more for it to heal. The perforation of the ozone layer was caused by "pencil-planes" recorded in the vision of Emma Kunz, an early twentieth-century Swiss-German healer and visionary. When you read her vision, remember: the US space program used Redstone, Atlas and Titan ICBMs to launch Mercury and Gemini astronauts. Russian ICBMs did the same heavy lifting for early Soviet Cosmonauts. All of these are nuclear weapons-carrying "pencil planes."

There will be planes shaped like pencils [missiles?] *that will take men into space and by so doing punch holes in the atmosphere, letting in lethal cosmic rays that will kill many millions.*

Pointed, conical shafted ballistic missiles next are described in the seventeenth century by Pastor Bartholomaeus as swords cutting the sky when entering space then splitting the earth upon re-entry when detonated over targets:

Heaven and Hell will confront each other in this struggle. Old states will perish and light and darkness will be pitted against each other with swords, but it will be swords of a different fashion. With these swords it will be possible to cut up the skies and to split the Earth.

Yeshua the Christ was the first, but not the last, prophet to define these future weapons as falling stars, for in truth, atomic weapons are man-made stars for a brief and terrible second of death when they stoke a stellar fusion furnace to incinerate cities:

Immediately after the suffering of those days, the Sun will be darkened and the Moon will not give its light [nuclear winter?] *and the stars will fall from the sky* [thermonuclear warheads?] *and the power of the universe* [the splitting of the atom?] *will be shaken* [nuclear detonations?]

Matthew 24:29

Nearly a millennium after Christ, St. Odile takes up the falling star story in 720 C.E.

A horrible warrior will unleash it, and his enemies will call him Antichrist. All nations of the Earth will fight each other in this war. The fighters will rise up in the heavens [rockets launching?] *to take the stars and will throw them on cities, to set ablaze the buildings and cause immense devastations. The nations will cry "peace, peace," but there will be no peace.*

These visionaries of world wars often remind us that there are *three of them.* Moreover, a civilization-ending danger of a third war is your clear and present danger. Visionaries like the Italian seeress Maria Tiagi in 1835 said:

At first will come several terrestrial scourges, as great wars, through which many millions will run into destruction. [30 million killed in World War One, 60 million killed in World War Two?] *After that will come the celestial scourge in full severity, such as has never been. It will be short but will cut off the greater part of mankind.*

To which Stormberger concurs:

In one day more men will die than in all previous wars combined.

The Sibylline Oracle of Babylon in the third century contributed more lurid, civilization-ending details enlarging on Yeshua's Mount of Olives prophecy of falling (nuclear?) stars in the Book of Matthew and Nostradamus' vision of the unraveling of the world of people and animals from the war of his Third Antichrist:

Then shall the elements of all the world
Be desolate, air, earth, sea, flaming fire,
And sky and night, and all days to one fire
And to one barren shapeless mass to come.
For all the luminous stars shall fall from heaven;
No more will winged birds fly through the air,
Nor footsteps be on earth; for all wild beast
Shall perish, voices of men, beasts and birds shall be no more. [Mass
    Extinctions?]
The world, being disarranged, shall hear no useful sound, but the deep sea
Shall echo back a mighty threatening voice,
And swimming, trembling creatures of the sea shall all die; and no longer on the
    waves will sail a frightened ship.
The earth shall groan blood-stained by wars; and all the souls of men shall gnash
    their teeth—the souls of lawless men, wasted by the lamentation of fear,
By hunger, thirst, and pestilence and murders—
And they shall call it beautiful to die,
And death will flee from them, for death no more
Nor night shall give them rest.

Pastor Bartholomaeus takes up the end time tale:

A great lament will come over all mankind and only a small batch will survive the tempest, the pestilence and the horror.

Nostradamus tosses in the mass grave a doomsday body count:

EPISTLE

The world will be so diminished, and its people will be so few that no one will be willing or in enough numbers to till the fields...two thirds of the world will fail [die off].

A third of humanity died in the first fire of blast and radiation sickness:

A third of mankind was killed by the three plagues of fire, smoke, and sulfur...

St. John of Patmos (AD 81-96), Revelation 9:18

A third died in the Great Famine following the world cast into darkness described in 1665 by a Scottish scryer known as the Brahan Seer. He foresaw a kind of fallout in rain from the condensing of a mushroom cloud unique to atomic blasts, as the people of Hiroshima and Nagasaki would witness and record 280 years after he presaged it; however, he's not talking about them. He may be talking about *us*.

The whole country [Scotland] *will become so utterly desolated and depopulated that the crow of a cock will not be heard, deer and other wild animals shall be exterminated by horrid black rain.*

Like Nostradamus, other seers share the vision of only a third of humanity surviving such catastrophes of climate change and nuclear war, two of these call to us from the land of Japan, the first victim of atomic bombs:

*Only one-third of humanity will survive cross-
ing the great mountain pass of time.*

Deguchi Nao (c. 1896)

If only one-third of humanity will survive it is better!

Meishu-Sama (1955)

Yet despite what are among the most horrific visions set down on papy-
rus, scroll or book in human history, there seems to be an alternative
future for which we should not hope, for hope is idle. We must ACT
decisively and create this future.

*Neither of the two adversaries will conquer nor be vanquished.
Both mighty ones [Russia and America?] will lie on the ground,
and a new mankind will come into existence... A great change
will come to pass, such as no mortal man will have expected.*

Pastor Bartholomaeus (1642)

*And the time is not far away, because the sleeping humanity has suffered
much and is going to suffer more, and as the suffering grows deeper...
it is a blessing in disguise. Man can tolerate only a certain quantity
of suffering and then wakes up. And man has suffered enough.*

Osho (1985) *From Darkness to Light*

chapter five

Stop Armageddon's Countdown
I want to get off!

History is a race between education and catastrophe.

H.G. Wells

N ostradamus provides two possible timelines for the length of Cold War Two before the terrible advent of visions from the last chapter. Let's first review the two verses:

4 Q95
The rule left to two. They will hold it for a very short time.
Three years and seven months having passed,
they will go to war.
Their two vassals rebel against them.
The victor is born on American [Armorique] soil.

Rule of the world left to two defines the US and USSR after the end of the Second World War. It's also a phrase bridge to 2 Q89 (*One day "the two" great leaders will become friends*) and a continuation of the prophecy dating the end of the First Cold War in [19]89, when: *The new land* [America] *will be at the height of its power. To the bloody one* [Gorbachev identified by his birthmark]*, the number is reported* [for the START treaty nuclear reduction].

4 Q95 continues the story. The two rulers, brothers/halved, in a short time after 1989 have a fall out, perhaps as soon as 1995, as the number

"95" comes up again in the indexing of similarly-themed quatrains (2 Q95, 3 Q95 and 4 Q95). The two vassals (*barbare?*) disrupt best-laid plans of US expansion defined in its own Orwellian doublespeak as "containment" of Russia. One of their loose-cannon vassals—Ukraine, Israel, or Saudi Arabia (American); Syria, Hezbullah or Iran (Russian)—act independently and precipitously, dragging their masters into a full-scale nuclear war at the time a new cold war is three years and seven months old. The victor is an American leader. How anyone could call himself or herself a *victor* of a thermonuclear exchange, given the horrible visions of Nostradamus and others, is hard to reconcile.

The next quatrain ventures a scenario of a longer-lasting second cold war before the dreadful globes set cities alight.

5 Q78

The two will not remain united for long,
Within thirteen years they will give in to barbare *power*
There will be such a loss on both sides,
That one will bless the bark of Peter and the cape of the pope.

Line one is a clear phrase bridge continuing the US-Russian brothers prophecy of 4 Q95: *The rule left to two. They will hold it for a very short time.* Line two with its *Barbare* anagram for Libyans/Islamic terrorist metaphor being "d'arabe" (Arabs), it is they who wield the *power* of unruly vassals from 4 Q95. That means the catalyzers are in the camp that includes Saudi Arabia (American), Hezbullah and Syria (Russian) *barbare*-Arab vassals, with North African Libya included.

This unethical, insane alliance of master to proxy, I predict, will be the source of a terrorist event, a Gavrilo Princip, shoot-the-Austrian-Archduke-in-1914 moment starting a new world war-turned-pyrrhic doomsday victory for the leader born on American soil (4 Q95). Victory might have annihilated Russia but the victor will lie mortally wounded and die later from the fallout of victory, if you will excuse the plutonium pun. As stated earlier, the last line dates this for our future times when there is a pope with Peter in his name, such as Pope Francis.

In *Nostradamus: The End of End Times*, I gathered the prophet's auguries that reveal his unsurpassed talent for predicting exactly the length of eras, periods of peace, war or tyranny. Yet he rarely gives a starting date for counting these periods down in the clear and leaves it to people of the future to recognize when to start a countdown. In my view, there are two ways to look at these new cold-war countdown scenarios, either they refer to two different wars or are alternative futures: either one rapid, or one lighting a longer, slower-burning fuse to Nostradamus' Armageddon.

If we take them as two separate countdowns then one could start counting at the official end of the last cold war, declared by George Bush Sr. and Gorbachev in December 1989. Three years and seven months later is July 1992, the time when the US presidential elections between Bill Clinton and Bush Sr. reached a climax. Bush would lose in November 1992. The man who promised Gorbachev no advance of NATO eastward converting former Soviet provinces and Eastern European satellites was out of office. 1992, as we noted earlier, was the year giving birth to Neoconservatism and its new hegemonic American strategic philosophy openly and successfully encouraging a gradual and aggressive NATO encroachment policy around Russia.

One could therefore argue that the new cold war has been going on since 1992 and should have exploded atom bombs 13 years later. The problem with this theory is counting 13 years from 1992 gives us 2005 with no nukes flying. However, we could consider the second countdown as disconnected chronologically and theorize that the 13-year countdown might be clocked after a dramatic "chilling" of this new cold war by some future incident, like the Ukrainian crisis of 2014. Even if the Ukrainian civil war is resolved or ends with the separatists winning or losing, the coolness of US-Russian relations might deepen as happened after the Berlin Blockade launching Cold War One, waiting for the next crisis to flare up perhaps years later. One could otherwise start the countdown after the long neocon-planned war with Iran begins, which according to Nostradamus' astrology, brings it on around 2015 through 2016.

I tend to favor the "alternative timelines" theory where we begin counting a new cold war arising like the last with a clear and definite incident or crisis as catalyst, such as the Soviet Berlin Blockade and the Allied Berlin Airlift. It may be a coincidence but when the American and Soviet governments tried friendship after the end of the Second World War, if you count three years and seven months starting from VE Day (8-9 May 1945) you get December 1949. The Soviets ended their blockade of all road and rail supply to Berlin 12 May 1949, exactly three years and three days after VE Day and just seven months off of Nostradamus' short count. The official end of the Allied Airlift was 30 September 1949, bringing the count much closer. Still, I think this interpretation is a dead end. If Nostradamus had described this conflict metaphorically as an Eagle fighting *Mars* (the red star) or an Eagle King (*Aquilon*) brawling with the *Hammer and the Sickle*, that's a different matter. Nostradamus made it metaphorically clear. Aquila the Eagle constellation represents the totems of both "kings" (read modern "presidents") or Brothers of the North. Obviously no war ever happened between America and a double-eagle, flag-waving Imperial Russia from 1555 to 1914. That *only* leaves us history in future tense from 1992 onwards, when a Russian "king" flies the flag of the Russian presidential double-headed eagle as his totem once again.

British Science Fiction writer and prophet H.G. Wells towards the end of his life despaired for the future of the human race after America lit off atomic bombs over Hiroshima and Nagasaki at the end of World War Two. He had grown starkly certain that humanity was set for a nuclear arms race to extinction unless a new "world man"—namely, a more conscious and rational man, who would apply himself to the challenges of life with scientific reason—didn't soon appear. Wells had already predicted the atomic bomb 36-years earlier in his science fiction novel *The World Set Free*. He had also foreseen atomic power possibly lighting and energizing the world, bringing peace, stability and prosperity but only if human beings abandoned what he itemized were humanity's "foolish dogmatisms and ultimate 'explanations' of life, the priestcrafts, presumptuous teachings, fears, arbitrary intolerances, tyrannies and mental muddles."

Before he passed away in 1946, he had written the following epitaph: "I told you so. You damned fools."

We are those fools.

We are those idiots who avoided nearly blowing ourselves to smithereens in October 1962 during the Cuban Missile Crisis, more as a result of blind luck than our conscious, rational intent. That was the closest the Soviet Union and United States came to direct, full-scale nuclear blows. It nearly happened because the Soviets goofed, secretly stationing intermediate regional ballistic missiles 99-miles off the US coast in Castro's communist Cuba.

The Soviet Premier Nikita Khrushchev often spent his summer vacation on the picturesque coast of the Soviet Crimean Peninsula with apparatchiks, family and friends. After a few rounds of vodka, he'd sweep his empty glass back and forth pointing southward across the Black Sea at Turkey just over the horizon. Launching a vociferous complaint, which in a nutshell rhetorically asked, "Why can't I put missiles pointed at the US from Cuba when right now they're pointing their missiles right at us from Turkey?"

Seems common-sensically a fair complaint, don't you think?

Do unto others as you would have them do unto you?

Therefore, Khrushchev put his vodka talking into practice and got one of the most unexpected shocks of his life. President Kennedy, who he'd met before and had reasoned was too young and inexperienced to act decisively, was decisive. Kennedy was even ready to wage nuclear war over those missiles in Cuba if they weren't immediately pulled out.

That's the problem about fools like us with our common, vulgar, just-in-front-of-our-noses, "sense." The world of humanity nearly ended because a Soviet Ukrainian projected an understanding familiar to any boy growing up in a land constantly threatened with invasion by powerful neighbors. Conversely, President Kennedy and all the president's men and advisors, congressional leaders, as well as the American people grew up shaped by a history never suffering the threat of invasion from powerful neighbors just over the border. Even

Pearl Harbor doesn't count here, because it was in far-off Hawaii, not a direct attack on the contiguous 48 states of America's homeland. With Cuba, Khrushchev gave Americans a dose of what a "turkey" time it is to have missiles aimed right off the coastline at you and nearly got his goose cooked in a nuclear microwaving.

The underlying thread of the tale of the 13-day Cuban Missile Crisis portrays Khrushchev and Kennedy trying to find a face-and-world saving way to pull themselves out of the terrible doomsday scenario Khrushchev's common-sense miscalculation had set in motion.

Kennedy was aided by a reading of Barbara Tuchman's *The Guns of August*, a history recounting the first month of the First World War. It's a cautionary account of so-called civilized European leaders and politicians unconsciously setting themselves up with reactive, trip-wire military alliances to keep the peace. When crisis came they carried out momentous decisions, blinded by nationalistic, knee-jerk, jingoistic narratives that fanned the rapid escalation of threats and fighting words that precipitated a world war that no one wanted. Tuchman's book recounts a train wreck of history that in four short years ended colonial European empires and set the world spinning and dizzy with communist and later fascist revolutions, all of which doomed the world to fight a second world war, followed by a cold war standoff and lastly led up to a test of Kennedy's "Cuban Missile" crisis in leadership.

He had read *Guns of August* in the spring of 1962 often reflecting about its lessons in meetings during the 13 days of the Cuban Missile Crisis later that October. By many accounts it had deeply influenced Kennedy's rationally prudent approach when dealing with Khrushchev's countermoves and often-contradictory and emotional communiqués. Kennedy would not be rash or rush ahead on assumptions; he would be mindful of his own patriotic blind spots and in so doing, perhaps averted a thermonuclear war by actually "learning" the lessons of history and not repeating August 1914.

Khrushchev had no history book to sober his actions. He had been a direct eyewitness and participant in Joseph Stalin's historic blunders. Miscalculating the American response to his missiles in Cuba no doubt prompted recollections of his days as a close confidant of the Soviet dictator. He witnessed firsthand Stalin's misjudgment about Germany's intentions in 1941 and the catastrophic consequences. Despite Stalin's blind obsession to the contrary and despite months of solid, actionable intelligence, in the end these reports proved that Hitler would attack and DID attack the Soviet Union on 22 June 1941.

When the invasion came, millions of Soviet soldiers and citizens caught unprepared would needlessly die in its initial stages because Stalin wanted to believe Britain was trying to provoke an incident with the Germans that would drag the Soviet Union into the war forcing it to join sides with the United Kingdom, for London's own advantage at Moscow's expense.

Stalin had misread the lessons of 1914. He was stuck in the past. He remembered how Britain influenced Czarist Russia to get into a war with Imperial Germany that it was equally ill prepared to wage. The decision ended the 500-year Romanov dynasty. He didn't want the British to trick Communist Russia into falling for the same trap with Hitler, bringing ruin to himself and his regime before the Red Army had completed its modernization and was ready to check a German invasion.

"We have taken Lenin's dream and turned it into shit!" remarked Stalin to Khrushchev in the initial days of the military disasters.

Khrushchev was witness to the turning of the tide against Hitler at the Battle of Stalingrad (July 1942-February 1943). Stalin had sent him there as chief commissar (political officer) of the 62nd Army making its heroic stand in the ruined city named after the dictator. Eventually, with the sacrifice of 1,129,619 Soviet and 850,000 Axis casualties killed, wounded and captured, the battle marked the beginning of the end of Nazi Germany, and the start of an advance down a long and bloody road Soviet armies took to Berlin. Where Kennedy's understanding of historic catastrophe was theoretical, though no less mindful, Khrushchev had survived the horrors of one of the bloodiest and most vicious battles in history punctuated by a closing, nightmarish memory. In the aftermath, he made a trip outside the retaken city to the snow blown steppes on its western approach where there lay great acre-sized heaps of frozen German dead stacked in high pyramids of 10 to 20 deep by bulldozers.

I've seen photos of the carnal fields Khrushchev visited with its high piles of stacked and half-rotting, half-frozen corpses, many stripped of their boots and trousers. A butcher's mountain range of corpses being pushed onto funeral pyres fashioned from railroad ties to feed the greasy black columns of smoke from open-air crematory flames.

A friend had asked him after the war if he had paid a visit to the burning corpse fields.

"Yes, I was there," reflected Khrushchev, his eyes cast in a faraway, grim stare.

"But I didn't go back a second time."

No one can know what his private thought processes were, what lessons or horrors he remembered when musing on working out a solution to the Cuban Missile Crisis he started. I like to think a memory of those flaming piles of humanity might have conjured a sense of greater danger. Let there not be a replay of the holocaust the Nazis had inflicted on the Soviet Union, only now with billions potentially piled for burning by nuclear war, if he would render decisions as blind as Stalin, insane as Hitler and not back down. He MUST pull out his missiles from Cuba. And he did.

Both Kennedy and Khrushchev had come closer than any other men in history to flipping a switch and destroying the world. We exist because both men rationally learned their lessons from history, studied or directly lived. The experience changed them. Khrushchev and Kennedy the following year established a White House-Kremlin emergency phone hotline, to better talk their way through misunderstandings before they would flare a cold war hot in future crises. They both pressed their countries to finally sign the Limited Nuclear Test Ban Treaty (5 August 1963), plus end nuclear tests in the atmosphere, under the ocean surface, or in space. These thoughtful leaders learned from their mistakes, put humanity and life first, political hubris second.

Conspiracy theorists will argue Kennedy's assassination a little over a year after the Cuban Missile Crisis, and Khrushchev forced into stepping down by the Politburo in October 1964 and put under house arrest, are the actions of special interests profiting from keep the US and USSR cold-war military industrial complexes in business. Both leaders may have become victims of those who did not want to learn from history's mistakes because they profited by them. Nevertheless, the seed to end a cold war had been planted. Ultimately Kennedy and Khrushchev's modest diplomatic efforts set in motion the idea of disarmament, then détente and at last brought about a peaceful end to Cold War One, albeit after another 26 years of military industrial profit-making momentum kept rolling those missiles out of factories.

Any men of lesser character, making decisions based on a less introspective study of past mistakes of history, might have destroyed the world in 1962. Are such leaders alive today to temper miscalculations in a new cold war era?

What do the world war prophets say?

In the second period will be peace, but only by name, not in reality. The tribulations will be as great as during a war... God will pour out the spirit of deception over them, and they will want what they don't want, will not want what they do want, and their actions will become so preposterous, that they will not be able to do what they are able to do. At noonday they will grope about like in darkness.

Pastor Bartholomaeus (c. 1642)

In our earlier investigation into this prophecy we tried out the "second peace" standing for a 20-year period between the First and Second World Wars, the "first peace" being the longer four-decade period from the end of the Franco-Prussian War and the beginning of the First World War (1871-1914). There was a "peace" of a kind in Europe between 1945 until the end of Cold War One in 1989. True, only fear of a mutually assured destruction could sustain a perverse peace, yet no direct conventional clash between NATO and the Warsaw Pact took place.

An alternative interpretation would describe this "second peace" as the chill of direct hostilities between US-NATO and Russia in a new cold war, perhaps the one Nostradamus foresaw as lasting either under four years or 13 years before World War III explodes. The description above of people living and doing things unconsciously, living in a haze of propagated irrationality could resonate with Stormberger's like-minded vision of a world like ours today.

Is Bartholomaeus trying to describe in more detail, a century earlier than Stormberger, a time when people and leaders alike walk into catastrophes with eyes wide open, reason switched off, in some kind of Zombie prophetic haze? Whether God or simple human stupidity pours out a spirit of deception, the native premonitory traditions all around the world express a shared concern that before the current humanity is destroyed by the imbalances of nature it has triggered, it will collectively go insane first. Right will be wrong, war is peace, hatred is love, in an Orwellian mind plague. Does it not seem plausible that we're under the influence of some gathering collective madness, when one regards the state of people and their leaders in America, in Europe, as we approach the mid-2010s?

They will want unlimited economic growth burning fossil fuels at an all-time high, but they don't want the global warming that comes with it. They don't *believe* the mountains of scientific data that prove climate change is human caused. The European Union leaders install draconian austerity measures doling out more economic pain and not a much-anticipated turnaround of economies. In other words, they will want what they don't want, such as job killing measures, dismantling the social nets, throwing more people into the streets who can't pay off the debt through increased taxes because they're unemployed. The leaders kill jobs to bring prosperity. Russia may be sanctioned further over the Ukraine crisis, even though it economically does more damage to the Western economies. No matter, forward ahead!

America wants to kill al-Qaeda but allows their economic and military assistance to easily flow into the hands of al-Qaeda forces to fight the Syrian Assad regime.

As I make a final editorial pass through this chapter in July, we hear and see on television ISIS invading Iraq from Syria and now America seeks help from Iran to contain them as it equally sanctions and contains the Iranians. Imagine the "idiotic-politick" of Iranian jets, someday flying over Iraq, bombing ISIS convoys, that is. They are blasting US "allies" fighting Assad, the Iranian ally. But Lo! ISIS drove into Iraq from Syria, thus becoming "enemies" of America's Iranian enemies, who might be American "friends" if they bomb and strafe Sunni insurgents-turned-enemy going over a border into Iraq. Just watch a Sunni rebel cross the Syrian border and he's no longer a "friend" killing Shia Syrians fighting with Assad. Over in Iraq they've become US enemies killing Shia Iraqi "friends." Oh yes! ISIS was never a US friend, even though we arm them in Syria... *and so the Stupid goes mad.*

Americans started this misery-go-all-around the Middle East heartland when it invaded and occupied Iraq to find weapons of mass destruction that didn't exist. There does exist unmanufactured materials to make chemical weapons and a stockpile of 2,500 rockets that ISIS seized from the tottering and divisive Iraqi government that America left behind. If they have within their ranks skilled bomb makers, it is quite likely that the Sarin gas will be contained in rudimentary warheads they could screw onto those rockets.

ISIS can't make an atomic bomb but they *can* manufacture hundreds of dirty bombs with that captured stockpile that includes radioactive isotopes. These would be conventional rocket warheads or artillery shells containing radioactive dust. Just one dirty bombshell fired from a captured US-made howitzer 20 miles outside of Baghdad lands in the government "Green Zone" where the massive US Embassy also resides. The explosion is minor. The spreading cloud of radioactive fallout over a square mile, will render the Green Zone uninhabitable for 60 years!

Consider the "maturity" of American leaders of our time who invaded Iraq on a lie that there were WMDs only to leave Islamic radicals of ISIS behind in Iraq, that even al-Qaeda disowned for their extremism and cruelty, with the means to create WMDs. Our leaders, when international crises will come, are not Kennedy or Khrushchev material. Indeed, we might have to consider the unthinkable possibility that the *barbare*-Arabs of ISIS lighting those Sarin- and dirty-bomb tipped 2,500 missiles are the rebellious vassals that drag America and Russia into a third world war!

These are our leaders. They talk to us in platitudes. They say "yes we can" and almost sound like they know what they can or can't do and we almost understand that we can't follow them for much longer without some terrible catastrophe befalling the world.

In the following verse, Nostradamus might take up this thread, pulled from the straightjacket of a maddening humanity, in these lines from yet another verse numbered "95." Once again he may be trying to date a time when things first began turning sour (1995) for the two great brothers, not yet brothers on a road to Armageddon.

2 Q95

The lands populated by humans will become uninhabitable,
Great disagreement and discord in order to obtain land.
Kingdoms given to men incapable of prudence
Then for the great brothers [US & Russia] *death and dissention.*

Read here many of today's land disputes that could fire up a Third World War in the near future, such as Russia's dispute with the US and NATO over the partition of Kosovo from their ally Serbia in 1999. It so happens the KLA (Kosovo Liberation Army) launched its guerrilla war ambushing Serbian police forces in Kosovo in 1995! Here too may be included Vladimir Putin's lightly veiled threats to strong-arm countries formerly part of the Soviet Union into the sphere of Russian influence. The lands disputed or to be obtained by force are the Baltic States, Ukraine, the Crimean Peninsula, also, the entrenched Russian occupation of Abkhazia and South Ossetia.

Georgia started and lost the five-day long South Ossetia War with Russia (August 2008). It is believed Georgian President Shaakashvili was encouraged by US and Israeli intelligence agents into shelling and invading the breakaway province of South Ossetia. The two had based special forces there as well, more to watch Putin's Russia than Chechen terrorists inside it along Georgia's shared border drawing a line across the spine of the Caucasus Mountains. Russian forces responded by occupying central Georgia for a few days, briefly cutting off the crude oil supply to Europe from a new pipeline running westward out of the

Baku oil fields in the Caspian Sea, demonstrating to Western warmongers how easy it was to cut off supply in the future.

Governing elites in the West put blind faith in the rules and regulations of international governing systems they believe have trumped and transcended what they dismiss as obsolete games of great powers past. They were soooo nineteenth century, those imperial European colonial powers, old fogies fixated on wrestling geography and resources from each other.

Guess what, you EU Brussels-sprout bureaucrats of the twenty-first century, the nineteenth century is back and on steroids. More than ever before nations maneuver with a vengeance to possess dwindling resources and establish a geographic advantage. Overpopulation and peak consumption of food, fuel sources and industrial materials is destroying the planet's ecological balance and making much of this overcrowded and polluted world "uninhabitable," just as Nostradamus may be implying as a first step to wars over geography and resources laying waste to lands by means of his foreseen "dreadful globes."

Follow theaters of international tension mounting over acquiring water and energy for national survival and you need no Nostradamus or Stormberger to show you where the next battlefields of a third and final world war are located. Over 100 nations are poised to fight wars for potable water. There will be land disputes between America and Russia's proxies in the Middle East leading to blows over Arab and Iranian oil fields and disputes between Palestinians and Israelis over water aquifers under the West Bank.

I say again unto you. Look at the men and women in power in our times. Do they read Barbara Tuchman? Have they looked Armageddon in the eye and witnessed the heaps of dead as haunting memories to stay the hand of missile launches in a new Cuban Missile Crisis? The world has given its kingdoms to the Bushes, the Obamas, the Clintons, and these imprudent men and women listen to the neocon-artist zealots like the Nulands, the neo-liberal exceptionalists like the Kerrys. An idle American people stood passively by in 2010 when the US Supreme Court sold off their humanity to the highest corporate bidders. The members of Chief Justice John Roberts' court have dispensed more human value to corporations than human beings. Can a US Constitution long survive such morally corrupt and injudicious men?

What circumspect men and women are our counsels, or diplomats and peacemakers? Did you know the US State Department has been undergoing a brain and talent drain since money has become the lingua franca for winning elections and staying in power? The choice diplomatic jobs and key ambassadorial positions are more than ever rewarded to the top campaign financiers. The Obama administration is on record as the worst when it comes to giving millionaires and billionaires important posts who have next to no training in diplomacy nor do they possess a deep understanding of world affairs. The career statesmen and women who are experts and best qualified for these posts are leaving for the private sector in droves.

US proxy kingdoms are handed over to people under the spell of impudent agendas. Netanyahu listens to the Zionist Supremacists in Israel. Obama bows and lays his democratic values in the desert dirt before the slippered feet of the most repressive tyrant in the Middle East, who has long been America's chief *barbare-Arabe* Arab ally, King Abdullah of the House of Saud of Saudi Arabia. US vassals Netanyahu and Abdullah draw war plans against Iran with or without official US government support, even though hegemonic circles in Washington do give tacit encouragement.

When I read into what Nostradamus has written in the phrase *Kingdoms given to men incapable of prudence* I wonder, is the prophet clued into something even more mad and aberrant? Are the memories of M.A.D. (Mutually Assured Destruction) fading in Washington? Might US leaders fool themselves, slowly, inexorably into believing America could actually wage a nuclear war with Russia and China with little collateral damage?

In Chapter 5 of *Nostradamus: The War with Iran—Islamic Prophecies of the Apocalypse* (second edition, published in 7 October 2013), I wrote:

Back in December 2002, the Bush Administration published its "National Strategy to Combat Weapons of Mass Destruction." This is the follow-up document to its paper on National Security Strategy. A classified version of the document signed off by Bush in September 2002 was leaked to the Washington Post, called National Security Presidential Directive 17 (NSPD 17). The Arms Control Association in April 2003 said the leaked paper authorized, "pre-emptive strikes against states or terrorist groups that are close to acquiring WMD." This executive order apparently merges the concern about these countries expressed by the administration in the NPR [Nuclear Posture Review] with the pre-emptive policy sanctioned in the September 2002 security strategy. It reiterates the need for a "robust strike capability," which will require the United States to develop "new capabilities to defeat WMD-related assets."

There are many ways to skin cats and skirt international treaties. If, in the end you cannot bring off a thing because the political will of your people falters, plan for another to do your doomsday excavation of Iran's underground nuclear sites after which comes the nuclear blow. The first ever request for sale of 100 five thousand pound GBU-28 bunker buster bombs armed with BLU-113 Superpenetrator warheads was authorized by the Bush Administration in April 2005 and shipped to Israel in the late summer of 2006. Israeli military sources maintain that Iran and/or Syria are potential targets for bombs capable of being refitted to carry thermobaric or tactical nuclear weapons, the latter of which Israel has in abundance.

When Barack Obama succeeded Bush as president, he pledged to dial back his predecessor's preemptive nuclear aggression that openly contemplated the tactical nuclear option in their strategic plans for waging preemptive warfare on rogue nations. In 2009 he gave a speech in Prague, Czech Republic, outlining a vision of a world without nuclear weapons, yet Obama's 2010 Nuclear Posture Review hedges on nuclear holocausts. His policy renounces development of new

*tactical nuclear bunker buster bombs. These were a cornerstone
of Bush's "robust strike capability" to nuke first and ask questions later whether a rogue state actually "was" thinking of
building atomic weapons. Obama's policy would swear off
preemptive attack on non-nuclear-weapon states, but there is
a catch, which makes Obama's preemptive nuclear stance no
different from Bush.*

*Nations that are compliant with the Nuclear-Non-
Proliferation Treaty are not under threat.*

*This is Obama's trippy way of appearing more moderate
by leaving the doomsday option wide open because it excludes
North Korea and Iran who he views as non-compliant. Israel
is also non-compliant. It upholds the double standard that
Western powers continue to ignore when planning war with
Islamic states. This policy hypocrisy is a fundamental rea-
son why defiant Tehran cannot negotiate in good faith with
America or Israel.*

Former Assistant Treasury Secretary Dr. Paul Craig Roberts believes
the above strategic policy changes won't limit Washington's left- and
right-wing warmongers.

He claims, "Washington not only has war plans for launching a
preemptive nuclear attack on Russia, and also possibly China, but
Washington has a cadre of people who advocate nuclear war.

"We have people running around Washington saying things such
as 'What's the good of nuclear weapons if you can't use them?'"

What indeed is going on in the thoughtless minds echoing such
irrational questions from the halls of the Pentagon, White House
and Capitol Hill? Dr. Roberts has long warned and reminded us that,
"these weapons are so lethal that if just one percent of the inventory of
the US and Russia were used, the death toll would rise to at least two
billion people. Also, if less than half of the inventory of either the US
or Russia were used, life would cease to exist on Planet Earth."

Perhaps Dr. Roberts lets his emotions or his memories of the First
Cold War days, spent in the White House between (1981-1982), get

the best of him. At that time nuclear stockpiles in the US and USSR together comprised a frightening 77,000 warheads of all calibers and types from 25 megaton hydrogen bombs down to little nuclear bombs in briefcases. Indeed, it was estimated in the Reagan Era that a full nuclear exchange had enough blast and radiation to kill all life on the planet eight times over. The greatly reduced nuclear arsenals of the mid-2010s have lowered the planetary life-ending devastation to perhaps less than killing everything one time over. Indeed, that fact magnifies the danger because some politically retarded minds now reckon wars can be won using a reduced number of nukes.

Dr. Roberts has seen the same warning signs of such ideas spreading as I have, since writing my first edition of the Iran book in 2007. The Obama administration's "talk one way and do another" augmentation of National Security Presidential Directive 17 (NSPD 17), could be stretched to include Russia as well, despite the fact that it is compliant to the NPT (Nuclear Proliferation Treaty).

"I have been warning about this for some years," said Dr. Roberts. "I pointed out years ago that the Bush regime had changed US war doctrine such that the role of nuclear weapons was no longer retaliatory to be used in the event of a nuclear attack on the United States. It was elevated to a first strike position. It is now our war doctrine that we can initiate a nuclear war on somebody we don't like, whom we think might not agree with us, or whom we think might be prepared to go to war against us. This doctrine applies to countries that do not have nuclear weapons."

Conspiracy theory? Let's review objective facts. American administrations since the last cold war encouraged NATO's encroachment and conversion of former Warsaw Pact and Soviet Socialist republics to put their forces right on Russia's frontiers. The Bush administration in 2008 positioned radars in the Czech Republic and anti-ballistic missile batteries in Poland. They aren't there to stop missiles from the Middle East falling on Europe. They're pointed at Moscow. Since early 2014 the US pressure is on to turn Ukraine eventually into a NATO ally.

The US has already offered to train and arm the Ukrainian Army. Washington aids and abets Kiev's civil war in the eastern

Russian-speaking provinces, and last but not least at the time of this writing (June 2014), a significant shift eastward of NATO military assets is ongoing in the Baltic States, Poland and Romania. It would seem that talk of NSPD 17 isn't limited to little Syrias and Irans anymore. The neocon hit list has put Russia on its schedule for regime change.

Dr. Roberts explains why:

"Russia is a country that is large enough and has sufficient resources that it could rise to the position to being a barrier to Washington's exercise of hegemony over the world. So, Russia has always been the target of this nuclear war doctrine. How are they implementing this? The United States is now putting, on the border of Russia, anti-ballistic missile bases, or ABM's. In the Reagan years, it was called 'Star Wars.' These missiles are designed for intercepting intercontinental ballistic missiles. So, if we were to attack Russia, and Russia were nuclear devastated and pushed the button and sent ICBM's headed to the US for retaliation, the anti- ballistic bases would shoot down the incoming Russian ICBM's and leave America untouched. The doctrine is now prevalent in Washington that the United States can win a nuclear war because we have the shield of anti-ballistic missiles."

This idea possessing feeble minds in Washington in 2014 is as dodderingly stupid as French generals in 1914 believing a line of men charging shoulder-to-shoulder with fixed bayonets can overrun batteries of new rapid firing artillery blowing them to bits. ABM tests over the years have consistently delivered mixed results. ABM defense is not a shield, it is Geneva Swiss cheese and it would seem Nostradamus yells, "flee, flee everyone!" from this crackbrained idea that it can shield one from a full retaliatory nuclear strike.

2014 looks more like 1914 but with a potential, civilization-ending multiplication of military miscalculations in today's version of the Von Schlieffen plan presented above by Dr. Roberts. For decades leading up to the First World War, the Imperial German High Command had evolved plans that utilized modern industrial advances in mobilization, transportation and communications that could supply and move huge armies, mobilized overnight, in a future war against France. Telegraph and phone wires were laid out. Train schedules to speed the millions of spike helmeted German infantry and their huge artillery guns were calculated down to the minute so that its military steamroller could sweep down through the Belgian frontier overwhelming the little country in days. Next would march in echelon a string of seven German field armies numbering 1.3 million men advancing on a front of several hundred miles, plunging deep into France in a southwesterly flanking maneuver to encircle and seize Paris.

When the war commenced in August 1914, this Von Schlieffen Plan, named after the German field marshal, Albert Graf von Schlieffen, head strategist and Chief of the Imperial German General Staff from 1891 to 1906, had become Berlin's doctrinal bible for victory. At last the theory would be tested. Once put into motion it utterly failed because of unexpected consequences fouling up its schedule. The kind of movement of millions of soldiers Von Schlieffen imagined relied too heavily on old-style supply limitations of slow moving advance by human boot and horse-hoof supplied food and munitions. The sheer size of mobilized forces overwhelmed the signal and communication services enough for armies to fall out of cohesion in their southwestward sweep, allowing a gap to form along the Marne River. This hole in the plan was exploited by French armies in the First Battle of the Marne, bringing to a halt the German offensive.

The Von Schlieffen Plan hadn't calculated advances in transport that the French might use to disrupt the timetable. The French forces that penetrated the widening gap between German armies rolled rapidly out of Paris riding on new-fangled horseless carriages. The entire Parisian taxi pool was drafted to drive the French soldiers to the front in their jalopies. The rapid deployment of this first use of motorized infantry was enough to break Von Schlieffen's spike-helmeted planned poke at Paris. Neither French motorized transport had been factored, nor had generals and planners on either side anticipated what terrible losses, harvested by new military inventions, would slow and pin down advancing armies. Even the lowly infantrymen said of the accuracy of their rifles in 1914 that human targets drawn into one's gun sight almost always fell dead or wounded when the trigger was pulled. Whole regiments rushing in massed, human-wave bayonet charges were nearly all but sliced down like wheat undercut as if by an invisible the sickle made of bullets barking from a lethal tattoo of just one or two gun crews firing the new inventions called "machine guns."

The unplanned consequence of old-doctrines being shot up by new weapons shot dead the freedom of armies to maneuver in the open. The armies took cover. They dug in for four long years of static trench warfare along a Western Front stretching from the Alps to the English Channel where there, and on other fronts, the slaughter of millions eventually broke the Russian, German and Austro-Hungarian Empires, thus ending European dominance of world civilization. The British Empire barely survived only to begin its decline and disappearance in roughly 40 years.

Nostradamus and others are warning of the consequence of history-ignorant American and NATO leaders planning to wage the oxymoronic "limited nuclear war" on Russia becoming a far worse miscalculation than a million Von Schlieffen pipe dreams.

Then for the great brothers [US & Russia] *death and dissention.*

Nostradamus (1555)

America may have a completely different destiny to engage, not as an aggressor and container of Russia, but as Russia's friend and teacher. So says America's greatest twentieth-century prophet.

chapter six

Edgar Cayce
And the Hope of the World

One could describe the gift of foresight as akin to someone who looks at the horizon after climbing up a tall tree. From there sky meets earth stretching much farther beyond the sight of people standing on the ground at the tree's base. A seer can actually spy what's coming before anyone below sees or believes it. What the arboreal augur reports is usually scoffed at or rejected.

Despite this incredulity, prophets and their interpreters must hold fast to an intuition received way out on a limb, peeling one's gaze deep into tomorrow—far removed from those below, leaning against the trunk of truculent attitudes in present time. The higher is your perch in prophecy, the more you hang exposed up there, bearing witness to things far above and waiting far beyond what crowds below can believe or comprehend.

I write this book living as an American. I'm nine months through my 58th year of this habit of counting myself among those programmed to call themselves "Americans." It has, over time and meditation, become a more utilitarian label for the corporeal shell around a "no-thing-ness" some call "soul." When I'm aware of *soul*, it is a paradox witnessing the body-mind in *life*.

It is like a bird.

It flies on unbothered and untrammeled by our make-believe boundaries fabricated out of fundamentally invisible-yet-psychologically imprisoning identities.

No bird or soul needs a passport, yet a personality does. It needs a flag too, and reasons to fight other people with different passports and flags as soon as the conditioning begins sinking into a newborn child's unwritten *tabula rasa* mind. The child must let others write on the surface of its soul identities like "man" or "woman," or "American" or something else, to survive, to belong, to be loved. These labels become one's prison identity ego-number, not tattooed on a forearm at Auschwitz, but tattooed in one's brain in a concentration camp built out of mindsets, barb wired by the idea of being somebody when a soul is a "no body."

Once there was an American living in the twentieth century; he used to lay on a couch with a lady stenographer and wife by his side as witnesses. He'd fold his hands on his chest, breathe deeply, relaxing... Going "no body" back to pure "soul" state. From there, an unsuppressed spirit climbed a greater Tree of Life and peered distantly into the future's potentials over the horizon. Another voice would pass through his reclined, entranced form and speak.

During his lifetime the stenographer witnessed and recorded over 14,000 trance readings, most of which answered letters about how to be healed. Detailed, documented predictions are scattered in these messages of healing and spiritual advice, often filed away years before their fulfillment. The man would awaken from his self-induced trances completely unaware of what he had said. Usually his first comment was, "What did we get?"

The Hearst newspapers branded the man America's "Sleeping Prophet."

His name was Edgar Cayce. He was born in 1877, a simple farm boy, shy, good-natured and deeply religious. He used to say he read the Bible from cover to cover once every year. His sixth sense was awakened as a result of a learning impairment. At the age of nine, his teacher called him an idiot because he couldn't spell the word "cabin" correctly. Nor could his father teach the boy the rudiments of spelling. One evening he left the boy's bedroom in frustration. Cayce later related that once left alone, he heard a voice say, "Sleep now, and we will help you." Cayce dozed off with his spelling book tucked under his head as a pillow. When his father woke him up thirty minutes later, both were amazed when Cayce could recite every lesson in the book.

A baseball can be thanked for awakening Cayce's healing powers. He was seriously injured when a childhood friend slammed a home run into his head. The unconscious boy was carried home. A trance-like voice stirred his lips, instructing his mother to apply a certain poultice on the nape of his neck. Cayce soon recovered.

He dropped out of high school after the ninth grade, married, fathered two children and scraped together a living, first as a clerk, then working at a bookstore and later selling life insurance. With time, word spread around the country about an uneducated country bumpkin who lay down on a couch in a hypnotic state and prescribed down-to-earth folk medical cures.

Eventually his stenographer documented a lifetime output of 14,306 readings. For years he refused to take payment for his work but at last his wife convinced him to take a modest fee from those who could pay. He offered his services free to the poor.

In 1927 Cayce moved to Virginia Beach, Virginia. Wealthy supporters had financed the construction of a modest hospital there. It's initial failure would evolve into a new center called ARE (the Association for Research and Enlightenment). According to the ARE website, the association is dedicated "to explore spirituality, holistic health, intuition, dream interpretation, psychic development, reincarnation, and ancient mysteries."

Edgar Cayce logged a number of accurate prophecies while talking in his sleep, many of them date stamped in future time: the hardest kind to get right. He's most famous for his "earth changes" forecasts about earthquakes, volcanic eruptions and the reshaping of future continents; however, his indexed and time-logged prescient advice to clients on the ups and downs of the stock market delivered more practical help saving many from losing their shirts in the Crash of 1929. Many also profited from his trance-induced counsel to invest again only after 1933—as it turned out, the year Franklin Roosevelt launched his New Deal and the long road out of the Great Depression.

On rare occasions he experienced conscious visions.

On a sunny afternoon in June 1931, Cayce was hoeing his garden with his wife. Suddenly he stood erect. The hoe fell from his hands. Without a word, he rushed into the house and locked himself in the study. After several hours he came out and explained that he had seen a vision of a coming world war in which millions of men and women would be killed. The transcripts of thousands of sleep readings during the 1930s would contain further and accurate dates and descriptions of the time and duration of the Second World War.

Cayce advance-chronicled the stages leading towards a Second World War as well. In the early 1930s his catalogued readings pinpointed 1936 as the point of no return to peace. That's the year Hitler occupied the Rhineland, the first of his string of land-grabbing gambles. A reading dated 1935 anticipated an *Anschluss* (absorption) of Austria into Hitler's Reich three years before it happened in 1938. Jess Stearn in *The Sleeping Prophet* relates:

Frequently, in reading for individuals, he caught the overtones of great events affecting millions. For instance, in August 1941, four months before Pearl Harbor, a young man, debating whether he should enter the Army or Navy, wanted to know how long he would have to serve. "How many years are these conditions [wartime] *likely to last?"*

"Until at least forty-five [1945]*," Cayce advised.*

In the first year of the war, 1939, he forecast America's entry into the conflict: *The only likelihood will be in 41... This too—if the people pray, and live as they pray—will pass.*

A reading indexed in 1941 augured peace *to be established in* [19]*44 and* [19]*45.*

Cayce's most dramatic vision of World War II was a vivid, technicolored dream foreshadowing the death of tens of millions in the Nazi invasion of Russia in 1941. At the time he had the presage, in the summer of 1941, Soviet forces were reeling back from the panzer onslaught suffering the swiftest, indeed among the greatest, string of military defeats in history. Two panzer encirclements bagged the

Soviet Fifth, Twenty-First, Thirty-Seventh and Thirty Eighth Armies at Kiev (August-September 1941) and later surrounded and destroyed another nine Soviet armies along the Vyazma-Bryansk front in October 1941. Cayce at the time could not have consciously known about the loss of millions in the first phases of the largest battle in history fought on a 600-mile front before the approaches of Moscow. These encirclements together claimed a half-million Soviet dead and wounded, plus 1,280,000 taken prisoner, soon to be shuffled off to POW camps where most of them starved to death.

So then, on this rare occasion, Cayce awoke from this trance session given for a certain Mr. "R" fully remembering every detail—his Book-of-Revelation-style symbolic vision fresh in his memory for the stenographer to record:

I saw that the man was Mr. R. Then I saw another horse coming, a very red horse. As it came closer I saw that the rider was Mr. R., but he had on a white and a blue armor, and there were hordes of people following him. Then as the two horses came together, it seemed that Mr. R. disappeared and the two groups clashed. The followers of the first horse were well-armed, while the others were not. Yet, there were such hordes following the red horse that they seemed to march right through the ranks of the well-armed group, though millions were slain while doing so.

The Germany military was at its peak strength and capability when it attacked the Soviet Union. It was a fact Cayce couldn't have personally known upon waking from his dream, that Soviet forces were caught poorly armed with substandard tanks and planes. In some cases conscripts, even untrained factory worker battalions, charged in human waves against German machine guns and tanks, the first wave carrying rifles the second and third waves following unarmed because there weren't enough weapons. The second wave would pry loose the rifles from the fingers of the dead and wounded first wave, charging on until they fell and the third wave grasped their fallen weapons and advanced. The men would sacrifice their lives just to move what were mostly First-World-War model Mosin-Nagant rifles close enough to the Germans so the survivors could shoot at them. Throughout the three years the Russo-German Theater raged, reports frequently described the stoic hordes of Russian soldiers counterattacking overstretched German infantry and panzer defensive positions, crying "Urrah! Urraah!" They became a human tsunami of roaring men and sound, climbing over mountains of their own dead to overwhelm the "White" supremacist "Knights" of Nazism at a cost of nine million soldiers killed and 14 million wounded.

Cayce foresaw victory over the horizon of the present when most predicted the Red Army would be defeated in weeks and the Soviet Union conquered before the summer of '41 was over.

Cayce was a rare American in more ways than merely sleeping on the job that produced accurate dates and forecasts. He wasn't blinded by his own country's hubris filtering out a message from the beyond, no matter how deep it ground against the American-exceptionalist grain. Beginning with visions in his readings as far back as 1932 through 1944, the final full year of his life remaining, Cayce anticipated Russia's pivotal role as America's future friend. It is a country without which the allies in the Second World War could not defeat the Axis powers. Perhaps even now, Cayce's prognostications of Russia contributing a positive influence towards peace was promised even as our times darken.

Like Cayce, I was born an American. By now you've read most of this book and directly experienced to what length my presented interpretations go against the American supremacist grain. It is not a new point of prophetic view. For example, here's a commentary on Cayce's predictions about Russia written in 1990, the year after the First Cold War ended, and published in 1994:

—ᴗᴗ—

In 1944, before there was even a Cold War brewing, Edgar Cayce forewarned Americans of the future to take stock of themselves. The hope of the world would depend on it:

What is the spirit of America? Most individuals proudly boast "freedom." Freedom of what? When ye bind men's hearts and minds through various ways and manners, does it give them freedom of speech? Freedom of worship? Freedom from want? Not unless these basic principles are applicable...for God meant man to be free...

What then of nations? In Russia there comes the hope of the world, not as that sometimes termed of the Communistic, OR Bolshevik, no; but freedom, freedom! That each man will live for his fellow man! The principle has been born. It will take years for it to be crystallized, but out of Russia comes again the hope of the world. [Reading] #3976-29 (1944)

When I first read this trance reading I thought Edgar Cayce might be a communist.

✓ Actually, Cayce envisioned a future that might shock both Capitalist and Marxist power freaks...Nostradamus [supports] Cayce's claim that ultimately Russia will be the catalyst for world peace and brotherhood. [Nostradamus was certainly not a communist]... he was a god-and-king-fearing royalist and wealthy physician.

This is not the first time I've been confounded by an extremely utopian prophecy. Being born and raised an American, I find this collective vision particularly hard to swallow. But I've seen too many fulfilled predictions cut through my outrage and assert their truth.

Nostradamus's sixteenth-century contemporaries thought him a bit of a loon for predicting the quick fade-out of Portugal as the maritime superpower. Adding insult to injury, he proclaimed that tiny, insignificant England would fill the superpower void for 300 years.

He was correct.

I stretched my biases to the breaking point trying to contradict the Nostradamian forecasts that date the beginning of the US-Soviet friendship around the year 1989.

This interpretation at least seems to be correct.

When I shed my nationalistic righteousness for a moment, I understood that it is lethal for our future if we believe our world must be run "American-style" or "Soviet style"—or according to any other national ideology. History is the witness to this; the Pax Romana, the Pax Britannia and now too, the Pax Sovietica—are all extinct.

Hopefully, the UNO will not become the fading rubber stamp for the Pax Americana.

But the Uranian [Chernobyl] jack-in-the-box factor may pop up at any moment and expose victory's deeper insights first to the superpower defeated in the First Cold War. Perhaps losing twenty-[seven] million to World War II and ten million to Stalin's purges has taught the Russians a lesson about war that America has yet to learn—restraint. Would Americans have been so eager to Rambo their way into Iraq [during the Persian Gulf war of 1990] if they had lost twenty million people to World War II? History does not forget that America is the only nation to use nuclear weapons prior to Armageddon and rumors of Armageddon.

Cayce closes his famous declaration about Russia's destiny by offering a challenge and a dose of compassionate criticism to Americans:

It will take years for it to be crystallized, but out of Russia comes the hope of the world. Guided by what? That friendship with the nation that hath even set on its present monetary unit "In God We Trust." (Do ye [America] use that in thine own heart when you pay your just debts? Do ye use that in thy prayer when ye send thy missionaries to other lands? "I give it, for in God we trust"? Not for the other fifty cents, either!)

In the application of these principles, in those forms and manners in which the nations of the Earth have and do measure to those in their activities, yea, to be sure, America may boast; but rather is that principle being forgotten when such is the case, and that is the sin of America. #3976-29 (1944)

Apparently to Cayce, if Russia is tomorrow's great hope, America will nurture her transformation. An economic marriage between US technology and Russian natural resources was foreseen by Edgar Cayce in 1932 during the Great Depression. The prophet cautioned a businessman: *Many conditions should be considered, were this to be answered correctly. You could say yea and no, and both be right, with the present attitude of both peoples as a nation, and both be wrong, for there IS to come, there WILL come, an entire change in the attitude of both nations as powers in the financial and economical world. As for those raw resources, Russia surpasses all other nations. As for abilities for development of same, those in the US are the farthest ahead. Then these UNITED or upon an equitable basis would become or COULD become—powers; but there are many interferences.* [These]...*will take years to settle.* #3976-10 (1932)

The prophecy reminds me of an interview of Boris Yeltsin by *60 Minutes* reporter Ed Bradley in the mid-1980s. At the time, the current president of Russia was party boss of Moscow. At one point in the interview, Bradley asked Yeltsin, "All right, what can we teach you and what can you teach us?" Yeltsin replied that the Americans could help the Russians by teaching them more efficient business practices and sharing their technological know-how. In return, the Russians could teach the Americans how to live a less stressful life beyond the neurosis of uncontrolled competitiveness. Indeed, Boris Yeltsin or his successors may be expressing the practical outcome of Edgar Cayce's prediction on future US-Russian relations, and may be the one most likely to implement it. The cross-pollination of the two ideologies could change the political/social structure of the twenty-first-century civilization.

If the First Cold War has a karmic bill for America to pay, its people will not suffer the same magnitude of shattered dreams as the Russian people have from the scandal called Soviet Marxism. Then again, the deeper the repentance, the greater, perhaps, the potential for wisdom.

Millennium Book of Prophecy (1994)
From the Chapter: *Is There a Bridge to Utopia?*

—⟋⟍—

Advance now, over the horizon twenty years, to 2014. Recall Cayce's waking dream about the knight in white and blue armor on a red horse. It's a symbolic vision bridge to Nostradamus' *Great Red* (horse) prophecy becoming one of the *Aquilon* "Eagle Kings" of the North. Cayce's shining white- and blue-armored knight on the red horse represents the colors of the Russian Federation tricolor flag where its two-headed golden eagle is affixed. To me it means his "Hope of the World" prophecies were never intended for fulfillment at the end of the last cold war. They give hope that the world might still embrace: that the current threat of a new cold war will end in reconciliation before missiles fly, murdering two out of three human beings on Earth.

In the next reading, Cayce is talking about the end of the Soviet Union as the beginning of this hopeful process:

[In Russia] *a new understanding has come and will come to a troubled people...when there is freedom of speech, the right to worship according to the dictates of the conscience—until these come, but still turmoils will be within.*
Edgar Cayce (1938) #3976-19

This prophecy is being fulfilled in our times. The renewal of Russia since the fall of the Soviet Union in 1991 is already progressing. Most significantly to start with, the Soviet Union lifted all bans on religious worship in its final days, ending the communist tyranny of enforced atheism as the state-sanctioned religion. The current Russian President Vladimir Putin can be an openly devout Russian Orthodox Christian because of it. Progress towards Russians enjoying complete freedom of speech still has a long way to go, yet while American First Amendment rights are steadily dismantled in the twenty-first century, Russia has advanced far beyond many of the terrible repressions of speech and thought under Soviet dictatorship.

Cayce, a devout Christian—though unorthodox in practice of his faith—seems to have presaged that first step taken by Russians back into the Christian fold. This second coming of Christianity back to Russia would best guide the New Russia at the dawn of a new Christian millennium to work some unexpected miracles of peace with its neighbors.

Perhaps the following trance reading indicates this future. The European Union and the United States might have to drop their restart of a new cold war. Perhaps it implies that Russian Orthodox president Putin might work miracles of Christian tolerance and forgiveness to melt the savage neoconned, neo-liberally exceptional and hubristic hearts in Washington when the days of saber rattling and sanctions have grown darkest.

On Russia's religious development will come the greater hope of the world. Then that one or group that is the closer in its relationship [meaning with Russia; in other words, The US and EU] *may fare better in gradual changes and final settlement of conditions as to the rule of the world.* #3976-10 (1932)

Russia's leaders might impress upon Americans how to behave like friends rather than enemies. Other unforeseen and surprising developments might sheath American militarism through a sudden lack of funding.

I predict Russia, China and other BRICS nations will soon abandon doing business in US dollars, consequently lowering the dollar's value. That will serve to magnify the financial burden of sustaining America's bloated Military Industrial Complex to a breaking point. The roles in Cold War Two will change. Roles have already changed. This time around the US economy, with its oversized commitment to military spending, collapses from the financial burden just like the Soviet military industrial complex did in 1989-1991. Maybe it's a wicked coincidence of history repeating itself. The creaking camel's back of the Soviet Union met the breaking "straw" of a decade-long war in, and occupation of, Afghanistan. Every day it looks more plausible that US militarism's collapse will somehow happen in part because of the strain of an even *longer* occupation and war in Afghanistan.

The source of the decline of the British Empire was chiefly financial. Its inability to fund its overextended imperium resulted in a softening of its more aggressive military policies through financial default. It dismantled its holdings and military bases, just as the US would be compelled to do if a new reserve currency worked like a money bomb thrown into the path of its hegemonic ambitions. Washington would have to downsize its neoconservatism, take exception to neo-liberal exceptionalism and rapidly come to its diplomatic and budget downsizing senses.

I predict a patient Russian leadership is waiting for just that sensibility to awaken. As we've already examined, Moscow has shown ample interest in working with the US and EU to back all sides away from widening a war in Syria through diplomatic talks with US and EU partners in 2013 and 2014. Such Russia-led diplomatic moves have resulted in Assad's regime dismantling its chemical weapons arsenal. Despite the new cold war threats, up to the time of this book's publication, Russia hasn't missed a beat continuing in 2014 its efforts to negotiate a peaceful resolution between the US and Iran over the latter's nuclear program. Russia presently (June 2014) watches a low-grade civil war in Eastern Ukraine fester while the US presses for more economic sanctions on Moscow hoping to escalate tensions that might isolate and hurt Russia. Yet despite these bullying affronts, Moscow so far does not react in kind. Russia continues to allow the US to ship its military hardware out of Afghanistan on an overland route to the Baltic Sea, down the very same bridges and roads used by retreating Soviet forces in 1989!

Perhaps by these examples of good will, added to economic realities, America's projection of exceptionalism becomes impossible to financially sustain. It might be humbled to lead by example and try living by its enlightened constitution as well as abandoning altogether the neocon manifesto's manifest hypocrisy:

> *Conservatives these days succumb easily to the charming old metaphor of the United States as a "city on a hill." They hark back...to the admonition of John Quincy Adams that America ought not go "abroad in search of monsters to destroy." But why not?*
>
> *...Because America has the capacity to contain or destroy many of the world's monsters, most of which can be found without much searching, and because the responsibility for the peace and security of the international order rests so heavily on America's shoulders, a policy of sitting atop a hill and leading by example becomes in practice a policy of cowardice and dishonor.*

> *Toward a Neo-Reaganite Foreign Policy,*
> By William Kristol, Robert Kagan (1996)

No neocon-inspired overthrow of Putin in a regime change, dreamed by exceptionalists in Washington, will fulfill Cayce's vision of Russia as a renewed Christian nation and hope of the world. Rather, it will end the world in one terrible night of thermonuclear death for two-thirds of the human race because American leaders under the neocon, neo-liberal hysteria may be the real monsters. They regard Russia and other countries possessed by Power with eyes demonically tainting reality, trying as they might to sustain a neo-imperialist extension of global supremacy their people can ill afford. Thus America seeks to use its last power, military force, before economic collapse causes it to lose its military grip on the world.

We can trust that a better future is possible because in no chronicle of Edgar Cayce's 14,306 readings is there a definitive prediction of a Third World War. If he spoke of a war beyond the year 2000, it was in the cloudiest of terms and not as a done-doomsday deal. Given his accuracy dating and describing the Second World War, it makes one pause and consider if Cayce in his "Russia Hope of the World" prophecies was channeling an anti-Third World War future Nostradamus, Stormberger and the other world war prophets couldn't recognize.

Cayce's readings give Americans a loving, though firm, counsel on how to behave and how to remember their own Christian moderation and temperance. Russia needs Americans to "listen" to its brother, not pontificate, dictate or threaten. It needs to humbly consider President Putin's statement uttered when the world gathered in peace for the Winter Olympic Games in Sochi in 2014, at the same time the US-backed Maidan Revolution violently overthrew the elected Yanukovych government in Kiev and set the world on course for a new cold war. These games actually were a peace branch offered, a presentation in celebration of what Putin calls a "New Russia" that need not be manhandled or judged by an "Old" America, still locked in a cold-war mindset.

I, as an American, understand what my fellow American prophet was giving all of us Americans, a loving nudge to embrace friendship and not enmity between Russian and American brothers of the north. "Fiend-ship" can only lead to civilization's downfall.

In God *and Cayce* We Trust.

He has proven himself in the hardest prophetic disciplines an accurate forecaster of the Second World War. This seer doesn't perceive a Third World War, yet he does visualize in such breathtaking detail an alternative future. The hope of the world in Russia is a promise of world peace.

Let us all live up to that aspiration and help make it so, through friendship.

THE END
(Summer Solstice 2014)

Other Books by John Hogue

ESSENTIAL NOSTRADAMUS

This is a rare little book giving you the skinny on a big subject: Nostradamus, the man, his magical practices and a comprehensive overview of his greatest past, present, near future and distant future prophecies.

—⚭—

NOSTRADAMUS
The End of End Times

Read John Hogue's last—and often satirical—word on Mayan dooms-day or "bloomsday" and first word on the many other significant and ongoing reboots of prophetic time cycles that a fawning paparazzi ob-session with the Mayan Calendar had overlooked and neglected while they are still transforming human destiny.

—⚭—

NOSTRADAMUS AND THE ANTICHRIST
Code Named Mabus

Explore clues to unlock the true identity of the man of evil, code named *Mabus*, the third and final Antichrist foreseen by the world-renowned sixteenth-century prophet. John Hogue plays prophetic detective presenting his evidence after a 25-year search lining up contemporary candidates whose names and actions may implicate one of them as the man who would ignite a world war.

—⬥—

NOSTRADAMUS: THE WAR WITH IRAN
Islamic Prophecies of the Apocalypse

Never has Nostradamus "come into the clear" like this, naming names, accurately dating events and places outright about a war in the Persian Gulf between America and Israel against Iran. Ships will be "melted and sunk by the Trident"! Is he speaking of US trident nuclear missiles, or, the mysterious trident symbol hidden in the Iranian flag? This war is dated to happen after an interlude of peace negotiations in 2014 lead to the worst region-wide conflict the Middle East has ever seen. Armageddon, perhaps? That depends on accessing Nostradamus' alternative future hidden in prophecies written over 450 years ago. Peace is possible, dated for the last dark hour before a war that will change the life of every human being.

—⬥—

NOSTRADAMUS
A Life and Myth

John Hogue published the first full-bodied biography of one of the most famous and controversial historical figures of the last millennium. He traces the life and legacy of the French prophet in fascinating and insightful detail, revealing much little known and original material never before published in English.

—⟋⟍—

KAMIKAZE TOMORROWLAND
A Future Fiction Story

Akio Sarazawa, a Kamikaze pilot, dives his bomb laden fighter 90 degrees through a gauntlet of anti-aircraft fire. His target is the rectangular mass of a US Carrier swerving through the Pacific to avoid his crash. Maneuver as it might, it can't escape. The flight deck rising rapidly before him floats on a wall of ocean, beckoning, as if it is a doorway. But moments before the pilot meets this portal out of life, he thinks how good it would be not see the future death of his homeland. He is wrong. A devil's sea has other shocking, touching and altogether absurd surprises waiting on the other side.

—⟋⟍—

About the Author

Author of 26 books in 19 languages, "Rogue" scholar, world-renowned authority on Nostradamus and the prophetic traditions of the world. Please visit him at www.hogueprophecy.com

Made in the USA
Lexington, KY
30 March 2015